Kaffe Fassett's
QUILTS IN IRELAND

20 designs for patchwork and quilting

featuring

Liza Prior Lucy

Brandon Mably

Janet Haigh

Judy Baldwin

Sally Davis

Corienne Kramer

Julie Stockler

The Taunton Press

First published in the USA in 2017 by

 The Taunton Press
Inspiration for hands-on living®

The Taunton Press, Inc., 63 South Main Street,
PO Box 5506, Newtown, CT 06470-5506
email: tp@taunton.com

Patchwork designs	Kaffe Fassett, Liza Prior Lucy, Brandon Mably, Janet Haigh, Judy Baldwin, Sally Davis, Corienne Kramer, Julie Stockler
Quilt making coordination	Heart Space Studios (Janet Haigh, Ilaria Padovani and Julie Harvey)
Technical editor	Lin Clements
Quilting	Judy Irish, Mary-Jane Hutchinson and Vickie Farrall
Designer	Anne Wilson
Art direction/styling	Kaffe Fassett
Location photography	Debbie Patterson
Stills photography	Steven Wooster
Illustrations	Heart Space Studios
Publishing consultant	Susan Berry

Library of Congress Cataloging-in-Publication Data
   Names: Fassett, Kaffe, author.
   Title: Kaffe Fassett's quilts in Ireland : 20 patchwork
      projects using Kaffe Fassett fabrics / Kaffe Fassett.
   Description: Newtown, CT : The Taunton Press, Inc., 2017. |
      "Featuring Liza Prior Lucy, Brandon Mably, Janet Haigh,
      Judy Baldwin, Sally Davis, Corienne Kramer, Julie
      Stockler."
   Identifiers: LCCN 2017008964 | ISBN 9781631868573
   Subjects: LCSH: Patchwork--Patterns. | Quilting--Patterns.
   Classification: LCC TT835 .F36762 2017 | DDC
      746.46/041--dc23
   LC record available at https://lccn.loc.gov/2017008964

ISBN 978-1-63186-857-3

Color reproduction   XY Digital, London

Printed in China

Page 1: Kaffe's *Shadow Play* quilt, thrown over his
shoulder, echoes the architectural detail of the castle
beyond.
Right: Liza's *Maple Leaf Medallion* quilt looks very
much at home in the elegant setting of Glenville House.

Contents

Introduction

Being hungry for any color I can spot in life, I was like a child in a sweet shop when I first traveled to Ireland. Years ago, I bought a postcard that summed up my delight at the intense spots of color to be found everywhere in Ireland. It was a portrait of an older man in front of a brilliantly colored house that he had painted all over with delightful patterns of leaves, flowers and birds, and surrounding large blocks of plain lime and orange. The postcard was pinned to my studio wall for years. When I decided to shoot my next quilt book in Ireland, I dreamed of finding similar individually colored houses as settings for my quilts.

We arrived at the house of a great friend, Judy Brittain, who has been living near Cork in the southwest of Ireland for years. She cooked for and housed us in style while we canvassed a ten-mile radius of villages to showcase our quilts. Ireland is amazing in having the most daring and outrageous coloring on its buildings. You have to hunt them out amongst the rows of neutral-toned terraced houses but when you do find them, they are unique. Imagine my great thrill when I came across a little decorated cottage, faded but with similarly jaunty painted details to that fateful postcard. As we arrived at this little gem, the door was opened so we were able to inquire about its history. The owners, Thomas Lawlee and his wife, invited us in for tea and Jaffa cakes and said it was painted by his father. At that point they produced a postcard saying the house used to be a famous landmark; it was the very card from my studio! As we looked closer we could see that it was indeed the same paint on the

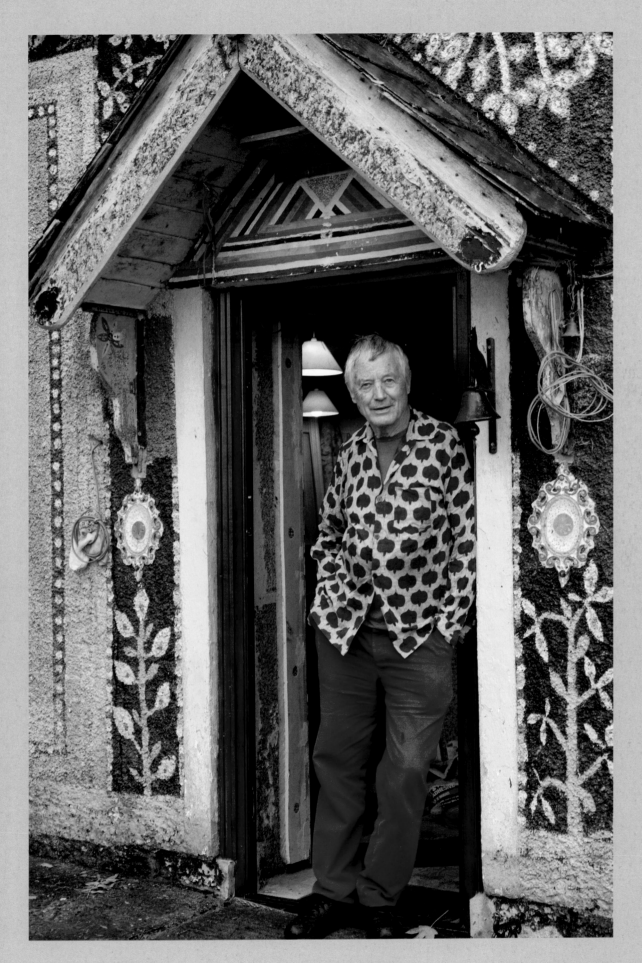

house – just faded by the weather over the years. It was the perfect setting for a pastel quilt and was such a strong omen that we were definitely meant to do this shoot in that part of Ireland!

We also were led by Judy to the great faded grandeur of Glenville House, where we were able to show some of our quilts in the richly colored rooms of the Irish past. How grateful we were that Silvia and Stefan Reynolds had kept the old colors and style of the house from its heyday. Funnily enough, as I designed my collection of new quilts for this Irish shoot, I visualized a grand room in a mansion with Chinese wallpaper on eau de nil coloring so I made two very soft green quilts. As it happens the color in our grand house was deeper and even more

interesting but I found a wonderful pale duck-egg green bakery in Cappoquin (in county Waterford). Not only did Barron's Bakery let us tape up our quilt on their shop front but fed us the most delicious orange cake I have had in years!

Because I knew we would find fearless bright colors on some of these Irish houses, I used a higher color palette than usual for several of my quilts. Our best find to show these off was an amazing greengrocer's shop in Mallow called Fresh Start. Their brilliant orange walls showed off the crates of oranges and bunches of fragrant carrots that rested on an electric blue bicycle outside the shop and was just the right setting for my Red Log Cabin quilt. I travel the world regularly and am appalled by the crass

nature of so much commercial signage, which really pollutes otherwise wonderful old town centres, so imagine my delight at finding such elegant lettering even on high street shops. I think Ireland is unique in this respect. Each time I return I am amazed at the standard.

Another aspect of Ireland is the lush green you find everywhere. We were able to place our quilts above rushing streams in dells, dipping into gorgeous ferns and draped over mossy outcrops of stone. A ruined chapel gave us the stunning setting of a vine-covered stone structure that showed off one of my darkest colored quilts to perfection.

Persian Carpet
by Kaffe Fassett

The brilliant jewel-like colours of my Persian Carpet quilt glow out from the ivy-clad walls of a romantic ruined chapel.

Green Diamonds
by Kaffe Fassett

This subtly coloured mosaic interior at Glenville House blends exquisitely with my Green Diamonds quilt, and the soft green paintwork helps to bring out the exact same shades in the quilt.

Chelsea Squares
by Kaffe Fassett

The elegant tones and delicate carving on this 19th-century
barn make our Chelsea Squares quilt glow, even in the rain.
This quilt should be a joy to make with its large-scale prints in
big sashed blocks. And it was our first chance to use our new
wider backing fabric collection.

Byzantine Lozenges
by Kaffe Fassett

What could be a better setting for the jewel tones in this quilt than a velvety old room in a grand Irish house? The red-robed figure in the gilt-framed painting and the dark wood surfaces are beautifully enhanced by the deep dried-blood richness of the unique wall colour. Another great colour find in Ireland.

OVERLEAF

Red Log Cabin
by Kaffe Fassett

This quilt positively dances in front of the orange-painted walls of a typical Irish shop front, with the electric blue bicycle providing the finishing touch!

Battenberg
by Kaffe Fassett

This is just the sort of rich colour one is so grateful to come across in the villages of western Ireland. Don't you think the happy tones of my nine-patch quilt do a jig against this scarlet door?

Contrast Brassica Snowballs
by Kaffe Fassett

I find it exciting to work in a strongly contrasting palette from time to time. Here I've used our black and white Spot fabric to set off our purple Brassica snowballs. It fits so well with the black and white lettering of a hardware shop in Cappoquin.

Shadow Play
by Kaffe Fassett

I could not have found a more perfect setting for this quilt! I just love the way the rusty corrugated roof on the bothy echoes the subtle changes of colour in the quilt.

Dancing Blocks
by Kaffe Fassett

It was the cobalt blue of these bound books that attracted me to this window corner. If I lived here, I'd be curled up reading in this setting every morning. The purple in the quilt is set aglow by these lapis blue books.

Floral Plaid
by Kaffe Fassett

This humdinger of a quilt with its clashing pinks and reds
meets its match pinned to the front door of one of the many
brilliantly painted houses in this part of Ireland.

Ripples
by Kaffe Fassett

It was the combination of pale green with the lovely corn dollies (an old British tradition in which decorations are made with wheat stalks at harvest time) in the window of this bakery that made such a good home for this delicate quilt.

Road to Ireland
by Judy Baldwin

The elegant repeating
mauve and green blocks of
Judy Baldwin's aptly named
quilt ping out from the
typically green and mossy
Irish glade.

Maple Leaf Medallion
by Liza Prior Lucy

This is the wonderful painted house that was portrayed on a postcard pinned to my studio wall for years before we came and found it for this book. Liza's poem of a quilt with its delicate, soft palette becomes a joyful part of the composition.

OVERLEAF

Pine Bark
by Janet Haigh

The elegant colour palette of Janet Haigh's intricately pieced, Japanese-inspired quilt nestles into a mossy corner of an Irish garden near Cork.

Hourglass
by Corienne Kramer

This handsome optical
illusion of a quilt is so clever
in its construction. I loved
placing it in the old library
with its soft green door.

Whirling Stripes
by Liza Prior Lucy

Liza tells me this quilt was inspired by a picture that antique quilt collector Julie Silber had pinned up in her kitchen. I love sunbursts in quilts and this whirling version lives up to form with its dusky palette. The fern-topped stone wall was a perfect setting. Who is the leprechaun we spotted in the nearby garden?

Garden Lattice
by Sally Davis

Sally Davis' mossy green and scarlet quilt becomes part of this stunning dell in soft autumn rain.

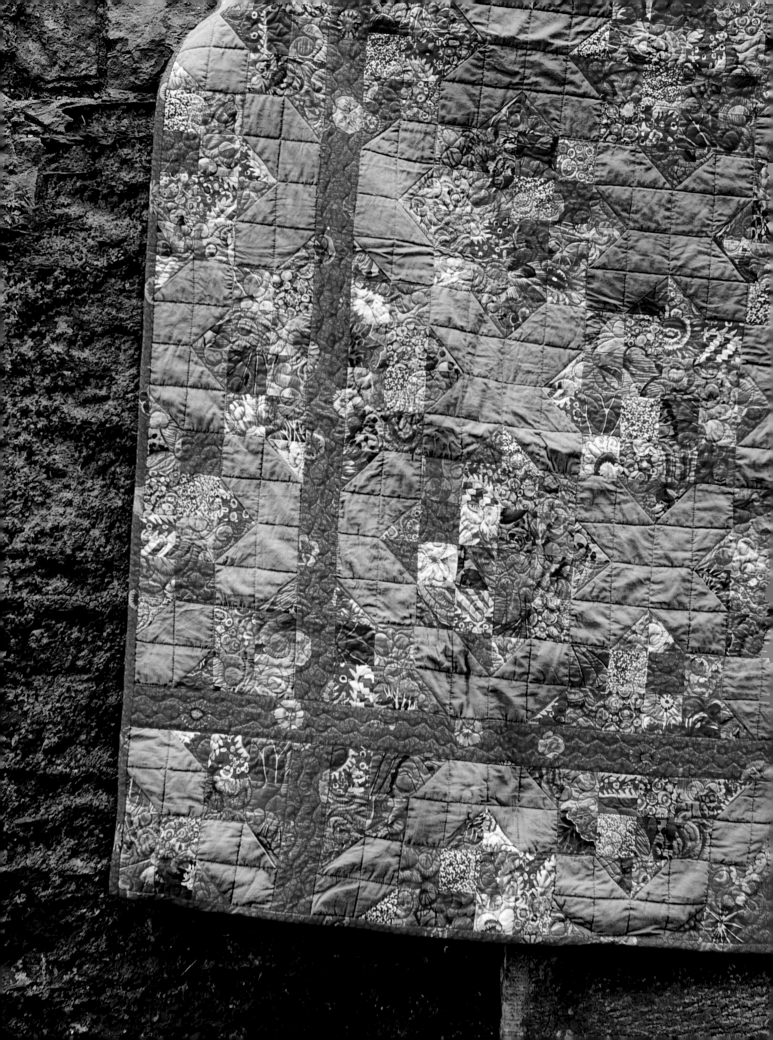

Eton Mess
by Brandon Mably

Brandon's Pinwheel quilt with its bold triangles and contrasting light and dark colours relates happily to a beautiful old Kelim in this Irish cottage.

Hugs and Kisses
by Liza Prior Lucy

Liza's playful quilt comes
to life on this bright blue
door. Its simple cheerful
graphics would make it a
great crib quilt.

Square Dance
by Julie Stockler

The delicate symmetry of this little painted church echoes a similar symmetry in the construction of Julie Stockler's lively quilt.

persian carpet *

Kaffe Fassett

This is an evocative medallion quilt with five borders framing a fussy cut floral centre. Every bottom border strip is slightly wider than the top and side strips. This display enhances the oval central design and gives the quilt a distinctive look.

SIZE OF QUILT
The finished quilt will measure approx. 80in x 86in (203cm x 218.5cm)

MATERIALS
Fabrics calculated at minimum width of fabric of approx. 40in (101.6cm), unless otherwise stated

Patchwork Fabrics
CAMEO
Wine   GP157WN   ¾yd (70cm)
PODS
Black   BM54BK   ⅜yd (35cm)
Wine   BM54WN   1¾yd (1.6m)
PERSIAN GARDEN
Black   GP160BK   1yd (90cm)
MUGHAL
Black   GP161BK   1⅝yd (1.5m)
END PAPERS
Black   GP159BK   1¾yd (1.6m)

Backing Fabric
CARPET
Black   QBGP01BK   2½yd (2.3m)
of 108in (274cm) wide

Binding
END PAPERS
Dark   GP159DK   ¾yd (70cm)

Batting
88in x 94in (223.5cm x 239cm)

Quilting Thread
Machine quilting thread

PATCH SHAPES
Based around a rectangular fussy cut centre panel this quilt has a succession of 5 borders of variable widths. In each border the sides and top strips are the same width, but the bottom strip is always 1in (2.5cm) wider.

CUTTING OUT
Centre Panel
Fussy cut a rectangle 15½in wide x 16½in long (39.4cm x 41.9cm) in GP157WN.

Borders
Some pattern matching is required for the longer borders (borders 3, 4 and 5), where strips need to be joined together – extra fabric has been allowed for this. Border 3 uses a fabric with large directional flower motifs, which run around the edge of the quilt. Make sure the motifs align with each other when you join the fabric strips and ensure that the directional motif is preserved when piecing the borders around the quilt. To avoid a quilt with uneven, wavy edges you may prefer to cut the border strips as they are needed, measuring your quilt across the centre horizontally and vertically at each border stage.

Border 1 Cut 2 strips 3½in (8.9cm) wide across the fabric width and 1 strip 4½in (11.4cm) wide across the fabric width in BM54BK. From these strips cut the following.
Cut 2 strips for the side borders 3½in x 16½in (8.9cm x 41.9cm). Cut 1 strip for the top border 3½in x 21½in (8.9cm x 54.6cm). Cut 1 strip for the bottom border 4½in x 21½in (11.4cm x 54.6cm).

Border 2 Cut 3 strips 8½in (21.6cm) wide across the fabric width and 1 strip 9½in (24.1cm) wide across the fabric width in GP160BK. From these strips cut the following.
Cut 2 strips for the side borders 8½in x 23½in (21.6cm x 59.7cm). Cut 1 strip for the top border 8½in x 37½in (21.6cm x 95.2cm). Cut 1 strip for the bottom border 9½in x 37½in (24.1cm x 95.2cm).

Border 3 Cut 5 strips 8in (20.3cm) wide across the fabric width and 2 strips 9in (22.9cm) wide across the fabric width in GP161BK.
Join strips as necessary (pattern matching as needed) and then cut 2 strips for the side borders 8in x 40½in (20.3cm x 102.9cm). Cut 1 strip for the top border 8in x 52½in (20.3cm x 133.3cm). Cut 1 strip for the bottom border 9in x 52½in (22.9cm x 133.3cm).

Border 4 Cut 5 strips 8½in (21.6cm) wide across the fabric width and 2 strips 9½in (24.1cm) wide across the fabric width in GP159BK.
Join strips as necessary (pattern matching as needed) and then cut 2 strips for the side borders 8½in x 56½in (21.6cm x 143.5cm). Cut 1 strip for the top border 8½in x 68½in (21.6cm x 174cm). Cut 1 strip for the bottom border 9½in x 68½in (24.1cm x 174cm).

Border 5 Cut 7 strips 6½in (16.5cm) wide across the fabric width and 2 strips 7½in (19cm) wide across the fabric width in BM54WN.
Join strips as necessary (pattern matching as needed) and then cut 2 strips for the side borders 6½in x 73½in (16.5cm x 186.7cm). Cut 1 strip for the top border 6½in x 80½in (16.5cm x 204.5cm). Cut 1 strip for the bottom border 7½in x 80½in (19cm x 204.5cm).

Backing
From the 108in (274cm) wide backing in QBGP01BK cut a piece 94in (239cm) wide x 88in (223.5cm) long.

Binding
Cut 10 strips 2½in (6.4cm) wide across the width of the fabric in GP159DK.

MAKING THE QUILT
Refer to the Quilt Assembly Diagram overleaf for piecing details. Use a ¼in (6mm) seam allowance throughout and press seams outwards each time. Check the measurement of the quilt each time before adding a border.
Starting with the Border 1 strips, pin the shorter strips to the sides of the centre panel, matching the centre point of the border with the centre point of the panel. Sew into place, easing to fit if need be. Add the longer strips of Border 1 to the top and bottom of the panel in the same way, placing the wider strip on the bottom.
Continue in this way to add Borders 2, 3, 4 and 5.

QUILT ASSEMBLY DIAGRAM

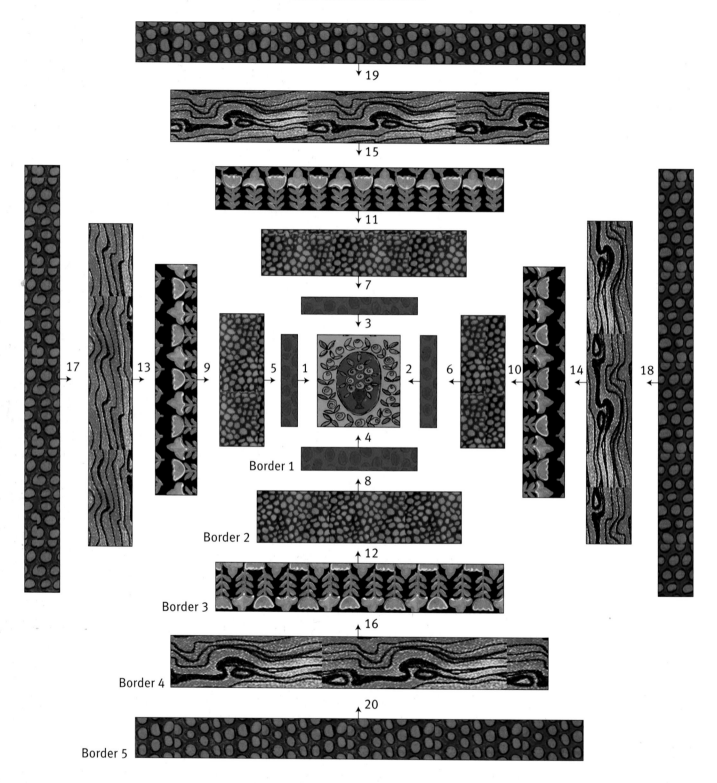

19

15

11

7

3

17 13 9 5 1 2 6 10 14 18

4

Border 1

8

Border 2

12

Border 3

16

Border 4

20

Border 5

FINISHING THE QUILT

Press the quilt top and the piece of backing fabric. Layer the quilt top, batting and backing, and baste together (see page 156). Quilt using a variegated thread to tone with the various fabrics. Stitch in the ditch of border seams. Elsewhere, freestyle quilt as follows.

Centre panel – outline quilt the frame, vase, flowers and stems.

Floral borders – echo/outline quilt the flowers.

Border 4 – freestyle quilt in selected black waves in the fabric.

Trim the quilt edges and attach the binding (see page 157).

 GP157WN

 BM54BK

 BM54WN

 GP161BK

 GP160BK

 GP159BK

green diamonds **

Kaffe Fassett

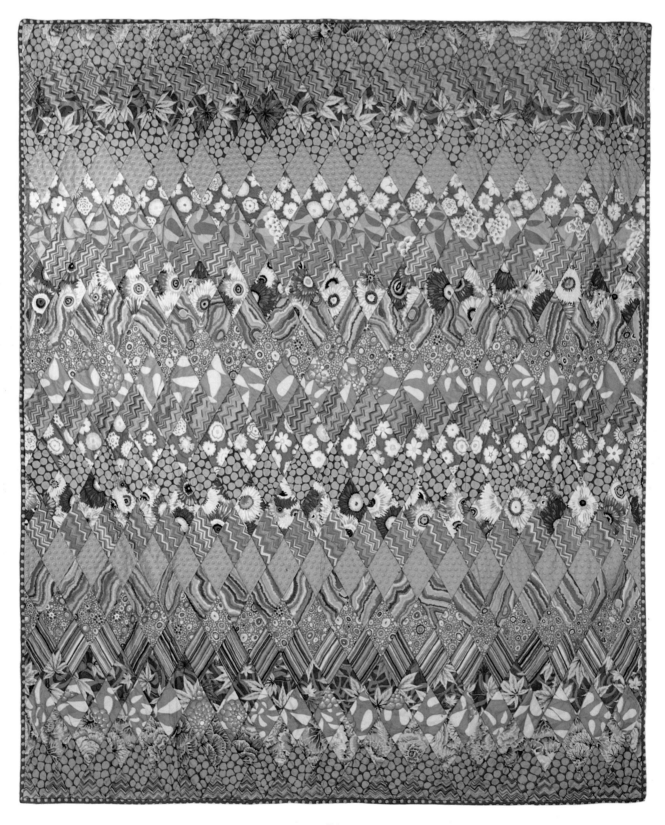

This quilt, using prints in predominantly green shades, is made using 60 degree diamonds, sewn together in an on-point layout, with side setting triangles and corner triangles. Careful cutting and positioning of the diamond patches will give you a delightful quilt, with interestingly angled patterns created from the cut fabrics.

SIZE OF QUILT
The finished quilt will measure approx. 65in x 77in (165cm x 195.5cm).

MATERIALS
Fabrics calculated at minimum width of fabric of approx. 40in (101.6cm), unless otherwise stated

Patchwork Fabrics
JUMBLE
Moss	BM53MS	½yd (45cm)
Turquoise	BM53TQ	½yd (45cm)

BUTTON FLOWERS
Green	GP152GN	½yd (45cm)

MAPLE STREAM
Mauve	PJ80MV	½yd (45cm)

ZANY
Soft	PJ79SO	½yd (45cm)

STRATA
Spring	GP150SP	⅜yd (35cm)

ZIG ZAG
Aqua	BM43AQ	¾yd (70cm)
Pink	BM43PK	½yd (45cm)

SPOT
Turquoise	GP70TQ	½yd (45cm)

VINE
Duck Egg	GP151DE	⅜yd (35cm)
Grey	GP151GY	½yd (45cm)

BRASSICA
Green	PJ51GN	½yd (45cm)

JUPITER
Jade	GP131JA	½yd (45cm)

ROMAN GLASS
Lavender	GP01LV	½yd (45cm)

Backing Fabric
CARPET
Green	QBGP01GN	2⅛yd (1.9m)
of 108in (274cm) wide

Binding Fabric
SPOT
Periwinkle	GP70PE	⅝yd (60cm)

Batting
73in x 85in (185.5cm x 216cm)

Quilting Thread
Machine quilting thread

TEMPLATES

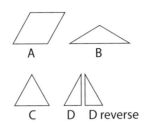

PATCH SHAPES
The quilt is made up of one diamond patch shape (Template A) and three triangle patch shapes (Template B, C, D and D reverse), which are used to fill in around the edges of the quilt.

CUTTING OUT
Template A Cut 3½in (8.9cm) strips across the width of the fabric. Each strip will give you 8 Template A shapes per fabric width. See the Diamond Placement Diagram for how to position the template on the fabric.
Cut 38 in BM53MS, 37 in GP51GY, 37 in BM43PK, 37 in BM53TQ, 37 in PJ79SO, 37 in GP01LV, 37 in GP70TQ, 37 in PJ80MV, 37 in BM43AQ, 37 in GP131JA, 36 in GP152GN, 19 in GP150SP, 19 in GP151DE, 18 in PJ51GN. Reserve the spare fabric for Template B.

Template B Use the spare fabric from Template A. Make sure you check the grain line shown on Template B.
Cut 4 in GP152GN, 2 in BM43AQ, 2 in BM53TQ, 2 in BM43PK, 2 in GP131JA, 2 in GP151DE, 2 in PJ79SF, 2 in GP70TQ, 2 in GP01LV, 2 in PJ80MV, 2 in PJ51GN.

Template C Cut 3¾in (9.5cm) wide strips across the width of the fabric. Each strip

will give you 17 Template C patches per fabric width, if the template is rotated 180 degrees alternately along the strip. Cut 18 in PJ51GN and 18 in BM43AQ.

Template D From the left over fabric cut 2 each from Template D and D reverse in PJ51GN and BM43AQ for the corners of the quilt.

Backing
From the extra wide 108in (274cm) backing fabric, cut one piece 73in long x 85in wide (185.5cm x 216cm) in QBGP01GN.

Binding
Cut 8 strips 2½in (6.4cm) wide across the width of the fabric in GP70PE.

MAKING THE QUILT
Arrange the diamond patches so a single fabric forms a horizontal row of diamonds across the quilt, referring to the Quilt Assembly Diagram (overleaf) for the fabric sequence. The quilt is sewn together in diagonal rows, so laying each row out in turn will help to keep the fabric sequence correct. The use of a design wall can help with the placement.
Using a ¼in (6mm) seam allowance throughout, sew the diamond patches into diagonal rows, adding Template B shapes along the sides of the quilt and Template C shapes along the top and bottom edges of the quilt.
Sew the diagonal rows together and then add the corners using Templates D and D reverse to complete the quilt.

FINISHING THE QUILT
Press the quilt top and the backing fabric piece.
Layer the quilt top, batting and backing, and baste together (see page 156). Using a machine quilting thread, quilt in the ditch. Trim the quilt edges and attach the binding (see page 157).

DIAMOND PLACEMENT DIAGRAM

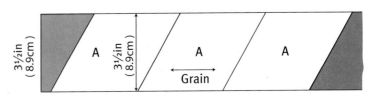

BM53MS

BM53TQ

GP152GN

PJ80MV

PJ79SO

GP150SP

BM43AQ

BM43PK

GP70TQ

GP151DE

GP151GY

PJ51GN

GP131JA

GP01LV

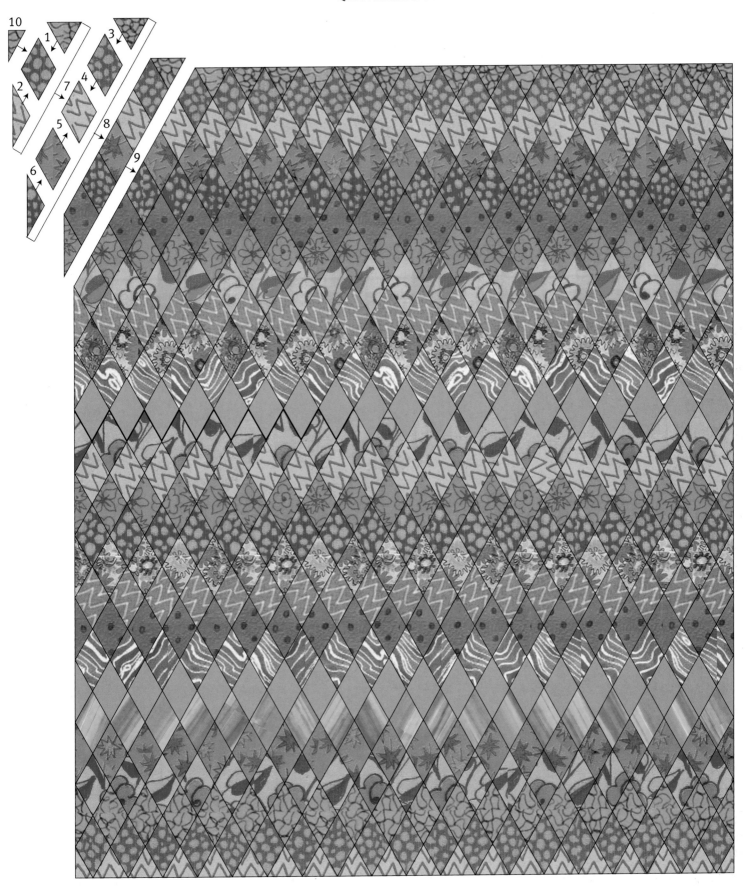

chelsea squares **

Kaffe Fassett

This traditional on-point squares design is perfect for showcasing some of the stunning floral fabrics from the Kaffe Fasset Collective. The floral print squares are arranged in a pattern with a general rotation around the centre square. Narrow sashing in a single fabric emphasises each square. Further emphasis is given to the quilt centre by the use of a single fabric for setting and corner triangles.

SIZE OF QUILT
The finished quilt will measure approx. 94in x 94in (239cm x 239cm)

MATERIALS
Fabrics calculated at minimum width of fabric of approx. 40in (101.6cm), unless otherwise stated

Patchwork Fabrics
LEOPARD LOTUS
Ochre	PJ81OC	¾yd (70cm)
Orange	PJ81OR	¾yd (70cm)

ZANY
Hot	PJ79HT	1⅛yd (1m)
Natural	PJ79NL	¾yd (70cm)

LAKE BLOSSOM
Magenta	PJ93MG	¾yd (70cm)

HENLEY
Orange	PJ78OR	¾yd (70cm)

VOLUPTUOUS
Red	PJ83RD	¾yd (70cm)
Green	PJ83GR	1⅛yd (1m)

TREE FUNGI
Pink	PJ82PK	1½yd (1.4m)

Sashing Fabric
SPOT
Fuchsia	GP70FU	1½yd (1.4m)

Backing Fabric
CIRCLES
Red	QBGP2RD	2⅞yd (2.6m)

of 108in (274cm) wide

Binding
SPOT
Fuchsia	GP70FU	¾yd (70cm)

Batting
102in x 102in (260cm x 260cm)

Quilting Thread
Machine quilting thread

PATCH SHAPES

The quilt is made up of one large square patch shape, edged with sashing. The quilt edges are filled in with setting triangles at the sides and smaller triangles in the corners of the quilt.

CUTTING OUT

Square patches Cut 12½in (31.8cm) wide strips across the width of the fabric. Each strip will give you 3 squares 12½in x 12½in (31.8cm x 31.8cm) per width of fabric.
Cut 8 squares in PJ79HT, 8 in PJ83GR, 5 in PJ79NL, 4 in PJ81OC, 4 in PJ81OR; 4 in PJ93MG, 4 in PJ78OR and 4 in PJ83RD.

Side setting triangles Cut 2 strips 19½in (49.5cm) wide across the width of the fabric in PJ82PK. Cut 2 squares 19½in x 19½in (49.5cm x 49.5cm) from each strip. Cut each square in half diagonally and, without moving the pieces, cut again across the opposite diagonal to make a total of 16 triangles.

Corner triangles Cut a 10½in (26.7cm) wide strip across the width of the fabric in PJ82PK. Cut 2 squares 10½in x 10½in (26.7cm x 26.7cm). Cut each square once diagonally to make a total of 4 corner triangles.

Sashing
Cut a total of 34 strips 1½in (3.8cm) wide across the width of the fabric from GP70FU.

From these cut 50 sashing strips 1½in x 12½in (3.8cm x 31.8cm). The remaining strips will be used for the longer sashing lengths as detailed below.

Binding
Cut 10 strips 2½in (6.4cm) wide across the width of the fabric in GP70FU.

Backing
From extra wide backing, cut a piece 102in x 102in (260cm x 260cm) in QBGP2RD.

MAKING THE QUILT

Lay out the 12½in (31.8cm) squares in the sequence shown in the Quilt Assembly Diagram, separating the squares with 1½in x 12½in (3.8cm x 31.8cm) sashing strips. Using a ¼in (6mm) seam allowance, sew these sashing strips in place.
Sew the rows of blocks together, adding a large side setting triangle to the end of each row.
Using a ¼in (6mm) seam allowance, make 2 sashing strips in each of the following lengths. It is advisable to measure the rows of your quilt before preparing these long strips, as your measurements may differ.
1½in x 14½in (3.8cm x 36.8cm).
1½in x 40½in (3.8cm x 103cm).
1½in x 66½in (3.8cm x 169cm).
1½in x 92½in (3.8cm x 235cm).
1½in x 118½in (3.8cm x 301cm).
Arrange the diagonal rows with the

longer sashing strips between the rows and sew these strips into place.
Finally, sew on a smaller corner triangle to each corner.

FINISHING THE QUILT

Press the quilt top. Layer the quilt top, batting and backing, and baste together (see page 156).
Quilt using a variegated thread to tone with the fabrics. The quilt shown was long-arm quilted.
Trim the quilt edges and attach the binding (see page 157).

Tip
When sewing the large side triangles in place, align the straight bottom edge of the triangle with the bottom edge of the row of squares.

ROW ASSEMBLY DIAGRAM

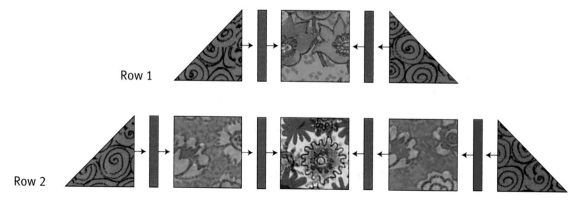

Row 1

Row 2

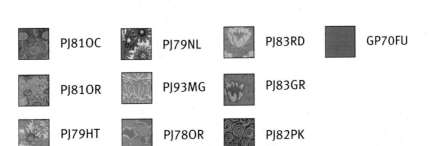

PJ81OC

PJ81OR

PJ79HT

PJ79NL

PJ93MG

PJ78OR

PJ83RD

PJ83GR

PJ82PK

GP70FU

byzantine lozenges ***

Kaffe Fassett

This stunning quilt uses a mixture of bright prints to produce a rich, jewelled effect. Set-in (Y) seams are needed to create this look. Diagrams show exactly where the prints have been used but the quilt is essentially a scrap one, so you could use a more random approach to fabric selection if you wish. The dark brown squares, created from 2 triangles, help to create a 3D illusion. Careful handling of the cut patches will make the piecing easier. A wide border frames the piecing beautifully.

SIZE OF QUILT

The finished quilt will measure approx. 63in x 63in (160cm x 160cm)

MATERIALS

Fabrics calculated at minimum width of fabric of approx. 40in (101.6cm), unless otherwise stated

Patchwork Fabric

BUTTON FLOWERS		
Prune	PG152PR	¼yd (25cm)
ZANY		
Dark	PJ79DK	¼yd (25cm)
PAPERWEIGHT		
Jewel	GP20JE	¼yd (25cm)
ABORIGINAL DOT		
Orchid	GP71OD	1⅛yd (1m)
TREE FUNGI		
Lavender	PJ82LV	¼yd (25cm)
Pink	PJ82PK	⅛yd (15cm)
BRASSICA		
Rust	PJ51RU	¼yd (25cm)
GUINEA FLOWER		
Red	GP59RD	¼yd (25cm)
Brown	GP59BR	¼yd (25cm)
Pink	GP59PK	¼yd (25cm)
ZIG ZAG		
Cobalt	BM43CB	⅜yd (35cm)
JUMBLE		
Tangerine	BM53TN	⅜yd (35cm)
Ochre	BM53OC	¼yd (25cm)
Blue	BM53BL	¼yd (25cm)
MILLEFIORE		
Antique	PG92AN	⅜yd (35cm)
LEOPARD LOTUS		
Ochre	PJ81OC	¼yd (25cm)
ROMAN GLASS		
Emerald	GP01EM	¼yd (25cm)

Border

ZANY		
Dark	PJ79DK	1yd (90cm)

Backing Fabric

ZANY		
Dark	PJ79DK	4yds (3.75m)

of standard width fabric

Binding Fabric

JUMBLE		
Blue	BM53BL	⅝yd (60cm)

Batting

71in x 71in (180cm x 180cm)

Quilting Thread

Machine quilting thread

TEMPLATES

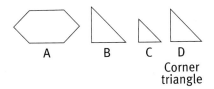

A   B   C   D
                                Corner
                                triangle

PATCH SHAPES

The quilt is made using one lozenge patch shape (Template A) and three triangle patch shapes (Templates B, C and D). Templates A and B are pieced into diagonal rows using set-in seams (see overleaf). Template C patches are added at the end of the row. Four of Template D are added to the corners of the quilt to finish.

CUTTING OUT

Template A Cut 3in (7.6cm) wide strips across the width of the fabric. Use Template A to cut the shapes. Each strip will give you 6 patches per fabric width. You will need 220 Template A shapes in total. The fabrics used in the quilt are given but you could use different combinations if you wish.
Cut 18 in BM43CB, 19 in BM53TN, 16 in GP59PK, 17 in PG92AN, 16 in BM53BL, 15 in GP20JE, 16 in GP59RD, 15 in GP1EM, 14 in BM53OC, 13 in PJ81OC, 11 in PG152PR, 13 in PJ82LV, 11 in PJ51RU, 9 in GP59BR, 6 in PJ82PK and 11 in PJ79DK.

Template B In GP71OD cut 10 strips 3⅝in (9.2cm) wide across the width of the fabric. Cut the strips into 100 squares 3⅝in (9.2cm) – 11 can be cut from each strip. Cut each square in half once along the diagonal to give 200 Template B shapes. Reserve the spare fabric for Template C and Template D.

Template C Cut one 2⅝in (6.7cm) wide strip across the width of the fabric in GP71OD. Cut the strip into 15 squares 2⅝in (6.7cm). Cut these squares in half once along the diagonal.
From the spare fabric from the Template B cutting, cut 3 squares 2⅜in (6cm). Cut these 3 squares in half once along the diagonal. This will give you 36 Template C shapes in total.

Template D Using the spare fabric from the Template B cutting, cut 3 squares 3⅜in (8.5cm) of GP71OD. Cut each square in half once along the diagonal, to make 4 triangles for the corners of the quilt.

Border

Cut 7 strips 5in (12.7cm) wide across the width of the fabric in PJ79DK. Join the strips together end to end. The individual border strips are best cut to length after the quilt centre has been pieced.

Binding

Cut 7 strips 2½in (6.4cm) wide across the width of the fabric in BM53BL.

Backing

From PJ79DK cut two pieces 71in (180cm) long and sew together along the long side.

INSET SEAM DIAGRAM

1

Stop seam
¼in (6mm)
from edge

2

Mark dots on
seam allowances
¼in (6mm)
from edges

3

4

ROW ASSEMBLY DIAGRAM

A → A   A → A   A → A

B   B

C →   ← C

B   B   B

MAKING THE QUILT

Using the Quilt Assembly Diagram, lay out all the patch shapes in the correct order. You might find a design wall will help with this. Carefully separate the patches into the 20 diagonal rows. The A and B shapes need to be sewn together using inset seams as follows. On the wrong side of the fabric pieces to be joined, mark the ¼in (6mm) seam allowances with dots. Place the two pieces of fabric right sides together and sew the seam, stopping ¼in (6mm) from the end (Inset Seam Diagram 1). Press the seam open. Take the piece to be inset and mark the seam allowance with a dot (diagram 2). Position the fabric and sew the seam, stopping at the dot, ¼in (6mm) from the end (diagram 3). Re-position to sew the final seam, from the dot to the end of the seam (diagram 4) and press. Continue in this way to sew the A shapes together, adding the B triangles.

Add Template C shapes to the end of the rows where indicated, using normal seams. Note that Row 10 and Row 11, do not need C shapes. The piecing order of sewing one row is shown in the Row Assembly Diagram.

When all of the diagonal rows are assembled, sew the rows together as in the Quilt Assembly Diagram.

Finally, add the four Template D shapes at each corner of the quilt.

ADDING THE BORDER

Measure the quilt across the centre width and from the long border strip prepared earlier cut 2 pieces this length for the side borders. Sew the borders to the quilt.

Measure the height of the quilt and cut 2 pieces to this length. Sew these strips to the top and bottom of the quilt.

FINISHING THE QUILT

Press the quilt top and the piece of backing fabric. Layer the quilt top, batting and backing, and baste together (see page 156).

Quilt in the ditch over the quilt centre, and then quilt lozenge shapes in the border strips.

Trim the edges of the quilt and attach the binding (see page 157).

PG152PR	GP59PK
PJ79DK	BM43CB
GP20JE	BM53TN
GP71OD	BM53OC
PJ82LV	BM53BL
PJ82PK	PG92AN
PJ51RU	PJ810C
GP59RD	GP01EM
GP59BR	

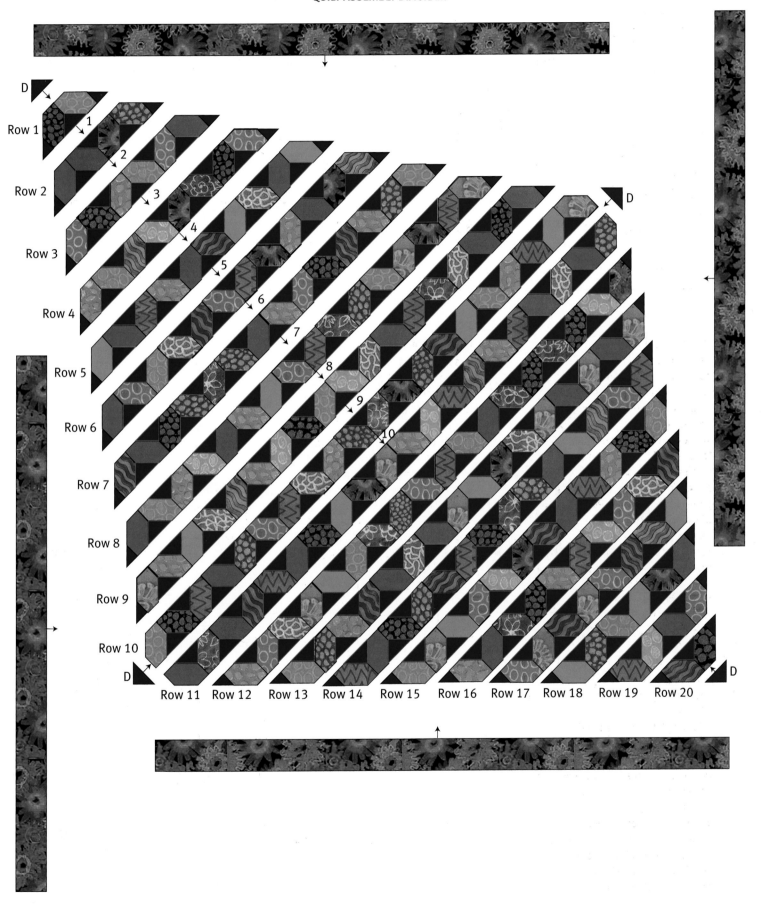

red log cabin *

Kaffe Fassett

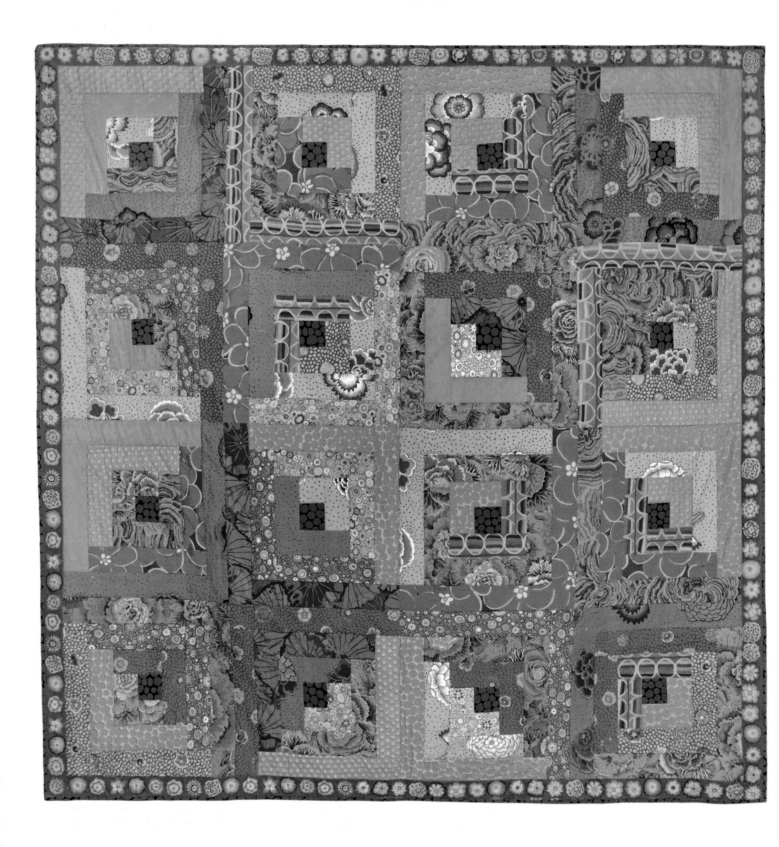

This is a scrappy quilt in the traditional log cabin design and is great fun to make. The use of two bold colour groups, one 'dark' (reds) and one 'light' (pinks), plus an electric blue centre square in each block, makes a stunning quilt that stands out from the crowd. A fussy-cut border showcases floral motifs.

SIZE OF QUILT
The finished quilt will measure approx. 74in x 74in (188cm x 188cm)

MATERIALS
Fabrics calculated at minimum width of fabric of approx. 40in (101.6cm), unless otherwise stated

Patchwork Fabrics
Buy ⅝yd (60cm) of each of the following, unless different amounts stated:

ABORIGINAL DOT
Shocking   GP71SG
GUINEA FLOWER
Red   GP59RD
Pink   GP59PK
PAPERWEIGHT
Pink   GP20PK
LOTUS LEAF
Wine   GP29WN
BRASSICA
Rust   PJ51RU
Red   PJ51RD
SPOT
Shocking   GP70SG
TREE FUNGI
Pink   PJ82PK
JUMBLE
Pink   BM53PK
Blue   BM53BL   ¼yd (25cm)
ROMAN GLASS
Red   GP01RD
Lavender   GP01LV
HEATWAVE
Tomato   BM55TM
ELEPHANT FLOWER
Orange   BM56OR
CORSAGE
Scarlet   GP149SC
Pink   GP149PK
BUTTON FLOWERS
Purple   GP152PU   1yd (1m)
extra allowed for fussy cutting the border

Backing Fabric
CIRCLES
Blue   QBGP02BL   2⅜yd (2.25m)
of 108in (274cm) wide fabric

Binding
JUMBLE
Blue   BM53BL   ⅝yd (60cm)

Batting
82in x 82in (208cm x 208cm)

Quilting Thread
Machine quilting thread

PATCH SHAPES
The log cabin blocks are pieced from logs (cut to size) around a central square cut 3in x 3in (7.6cm x 7.6cm). The blocks are then arranged in the traditional Sunshine and Shadows layout.

CUTTING OUT
This is a scrappy quilt so it is not necessary to place each fabric as in the original, just make sure the 'dark' fabrics are on one side of the block, and the 'light' fabrics are on the other. Start sewing with a light fabric first as this will make the dark fabric the last row, making it more dominant. The contrast fabric is the central square in each block. Take care when choosing where to place your blocks that the same fabric in the outer log rows 11 and 12 are not placed next to one another in the final layout. Use BM53BL for all the centre squares of the blocks.

Centre Squares Cut 3in (7.6cm) strips across the width of the fabric. Sub-cut into 3in (7.6cm) squares. Each strip will give you 13 squares per fabric width. Cut 16 in BM53BL.

Light and Dark Fabrics Cut 3in (7.6cm) strips across the width of the fabric. Refer to the Block Assembly Diagram and cut the fabric in pairs of logs, so that the same fabric is used in each 'L' on either side of the centre. See the Quilt Assembly Diagram Key for lights and darks.

Cut 16 pairs of light logs in the following sizes:

Log 1, 3in (7.6cm) long; log 2, 5½in (14cm) long.

Log 5, 8in (20.3cm) long; log 6, 10½in (26.7cm) long.

Log 9, 13in (33cm) long; log 10, 15½in (39.4cm) long.

Cut 16 pairs of dark logs in the following sizes:

Log 3, 5½in (14cm) long; log 4, 8in (20.3cm) long.

Log 7, 10½in (26.7cm) long; log 8, 13in (33cm) long.

Log 11, 15½in (39.4cm) long; log 12, 18in (45.7cm) long.

Border

This is made from fussy cutting the row of flowers in GP152PU to make a 2in (5cm) border (finished). Cut 8 strips 2½in (6.4cm) across the width of the fabric, making sure the flowers are central within the strips.

Backing

In QBGP02BL cut a piece 84in x 84in (213.3cm x 213.3cm).

Binding

Cut 8 strips 2½in (6.4cm) across the width of the fabric in BM53BL.

MAKING THE BLOCKS

Use a ¼in (6mm) seam allowance throughout. Piece the log cabin blocks, adding the logs in numerical order from the block centre outwards, as shown in the Block Assembly Diagram. Remember to use the same fabric in each 'L' on either side of the centre. Each block should be 18in x 18in (45.7cm x 45.7cm) unfinished. Make 16 blocks in total.

MAKING THE QUILT

Arrange the 16 blocks in a 4 x 4 block layout, in the arrangement shown in the Quilt Assembly Diagram, rotating some blocks as needed to achieve the dark/ light pattern and avoid two of the same

BLOCK ASSEMBLY DIAGRAM

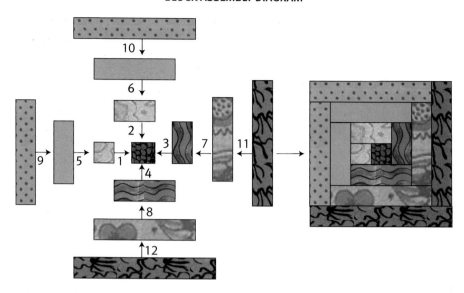

fabrics touching. Sew the blocks into rows and then sew the rows together.

ADDING THE BORDER

Piece the border strips carefully, matching the pattern at any seams. Place the strips so that a flower ends at both ends. Using a ¼in (6mm) seam allowance, sew the borders to the top and bottom of the quilt and then add the side borders. The quilt should now measure 74½in x 74½in (189.2cm x 189.2cm).

FINISHING THE QUILT

Press the quilt top and the piece of backing fabric.

Layer the quilt top, batting and backing, and baste together (see page 156).

Using machine quilting thread, quilt in the ditch.

Trim the quilt edges and attach the binding (see page 157).

> **Tip**
> Using a design wall for the blocks can help with the fabric choices and block placement.

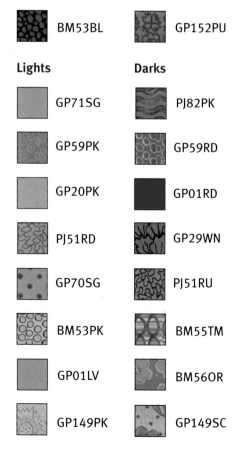

BM53BL	GP152PU
Lights	**Darks**
GP71SG	PJ82PK
GP59PK	GP59RD
GP20PK	GP01RD
PJ51RD	GP29WN
GP70SG	PJ51RU
BM53PK	BM55TM
GP01LV	BM56OR
GP149PK	GP149SC

QUILT ASSEMBLY DIAGRAM

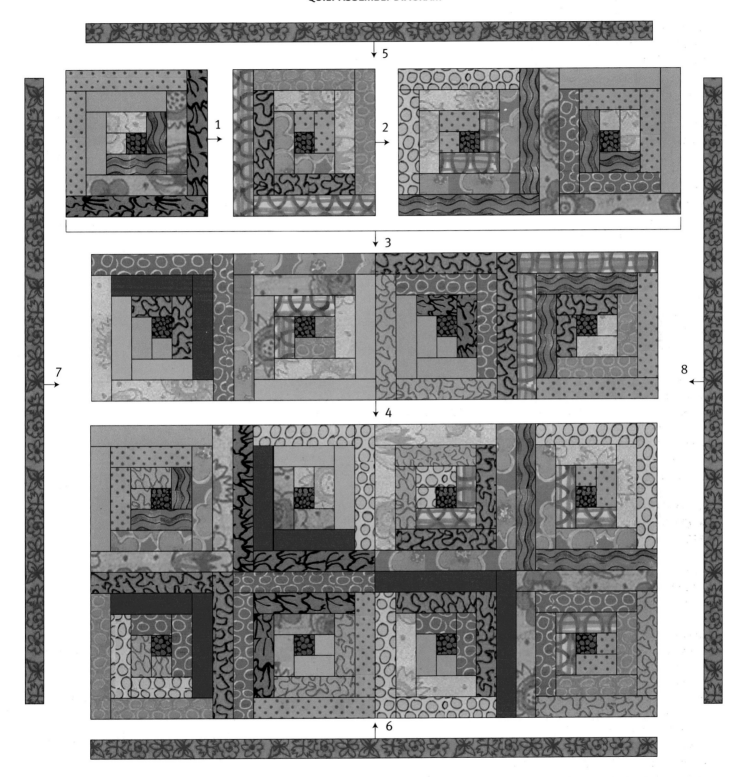

battenberg *

Kaffe Fassett

This scrappy quilt is a good one for beginners. It is made of 30 large blocks, each one made up of 9-patch units and plain squares. It relies on the use of the alternating contrasting blocks for its glowing impact. The fabrics used are mainly Classics and for ease of construction they have been divided into three groups – dark, medium and light. You do not need to place each fabric exactly as in the original, but we have given fabric quantities as a guide.

SIZE OF QUILT
The finished quilt will measure approx. 67½in x 81in (171.5cm x 205.5cm)

MATERIALS
Fabrics calculated at minimum width of fabric of approx. 40in (101.6cm), unless otherwise stated

Patchwork Fabrics
Dark fabrics
⅜yd (35cm) each of the following:

GUINEA FLOWER		
Purple	GP59PU	
STRATA		
Red	GP150RD	
MAD PLAID		
Cobalt	GP37CB	
PAPERWEIGHT		
Cobalt	GP20CB	
Jewel	GP20JE	
ZIG ZAG		
Cobalt	BM43CB	
Warm	BM43WM	
SPOT		
Magenta	GP70MG	
Peacock	GP70PC	
ROMAN GLASS		
Red	GP01RD	

Medium Fabrics
⅜yd (35cm) each of the following:

GUINEA FLOWER		
Pink	GP59PK	
Apricot	GP59AP	
STRATA		
Winter	GP150WI	
ZIG ZAG		
Aqua	BM43AQ	
SPOT		
Paprika	GP70PP	
ROMAN GLASS		
Gold	GP01GD	
Pink	GP01PK	

Light fabrics
⅜yd (35cm) each of the following:

SPOT		
Duck Egg	GP70DE	
Gold	GP70GD	
MAD PLAID		
Grey	BM37GY	
Mauve	BM37MV	
PAPERWEIGHT		
Gold	GP20GD	
ROMAN GLASS		
Pastel	GP01PT	
ZIG ZAG		
Grey	BM43GY	
GUINEA FLOWER		
Mauve	GP59MV	

Backing Fabric
CARPET
Red   QBGP01RD   2⅛yd (2m) of 108in (274cm) wide fabric

Binding
ZIG ZAG
Aqua   BM43AQ   ⅝yd (60cm)

Batting
75in x 89in (190.5cm x 226cm)

Quilting Thread
Machine quilting thread

PATCH SHAPES
The quilt is pieced using 2 different blocks, A and B, each measuring 14in x 14in (35.5cm x 35.5cm) (unfinished).

Block A (15 in the quilt) alternates 4 single lighter 5in x 5in (12.7cm x 12.7cm) squares with 5 9-patch 5in x 5in (12.7cm x 12.7cm) squares.

Block B (15 in the quilt) alternates 5 single darker 5in x 5in (12.7cm x 12.7cm) squares with 4 9-patch 5in x 5in (12.7cm x 12.7cm) squares.
Two contrasting fabrics make each 9-patch square. The choice of fabrics for all the 9-patch squares is random.

As a general rule each large square of a 9-patch block uses one predominantly darker or lighter single fabric.
There are 135 9-patch squares in total.
There are 135 plain squares in total – 45 dark, 38 medium and 52 light.

CUTTING OUT
The information below gives the quantities of individual fabrics used in the quilt shown, but the Block Assembly Diagram is set out as a scrappy layout, using light, medium and dark squares. You have free rein over the fabric placement and choice as long as you keep to the general contrast system of the two blocks. Note: the medium fabrics in the two different blocks can act as light or dark, depending on the placement.

Large squares Cut 5in (12.7cm) wide strips across the width of the fabric. Each strip will give 8 patches per width.
For Block A, cut 5in (12.7cm) squares – 52 in lighter fabrics and 8 in medium fabrics in sets of 4 matching fabrics. Total of 60 squares.
For Block B, cut 5in (12.7cm) squares – 45 in darker fabric and 30 in medium fabrics in sets of 5 matching fabrics. Total of 75 squares.

Small squares for 9-patches Cut 2in (5cm) wide strips across the width of the fabric. Each strip will give you 20 patches per width.
For each Block A, cut 25 squares in darker fabrics in sets of 5 matching fabrics and 20 squares in lighter fabrics in sets of 4 matching fabrics.
For each Block B, cut 20 squares in lighter fabrics in sets of 5 matching fabrics and 16 squares in darker fabrics in sets of 4 matching fabrics.
You will need 1215 2in x 2in (5cm x 5cm) squares in total in the quilt.

Backing
In QBGP01RD cut one piece 75in x 89in (190.5cm x 226cm).

MAKING THE BLOCKS

Block A Use a ¼in (6mm) seam allowance throughout. Make a 9-patch square as shown in the Block A Assembly Diagram, choosing 5 dark and 4 light 2in x 2in (5cm x 5cm) squares (diagram 1). Repeat to make 5 9-patch squares. Choose 4 single fabric light 5in x 5in (12.7cm x 12.7cm) squares and piece together with the 9-patch squares as shown in diagram 2. Check the block is 14in (35.5cm) square.
Make 15 of Block A in total.

Block B Make a 9-patch square as shown in the Block B Assembly Diagram, choosing 4 dark and 5 light 2in x 2in (5cm x 5cm) squares (diagram 1). Repeat to make 4 9-patch squares. Choose 5 single fabric light 5in x 5in (12.7cm x 12.7cm) squares and piece together with the 9-patch squares as shown in diagram 2. Check the block is 14in (35.5cm) square.
Make 15 of Block B in total.

MAKING THE QUILT

Use a ¼in (6mm) seam allowance throughout. Starting with Block A, sew the blocks into 6 rows of 5 blocks, alternating Blocks A and B following the Quilt Assembly Diagram. Now join the rows together and press.

FINISHING THE QUILT

Press the quilt top and the piece of backing fabric.
Layer the quilt top, batting and backing, and baste together (see page 156). Use a thread that blends with the fabric, stitch diagonal lines in each direction across the 9-patch blocks and the single fabric squares to form large diamonds.
Trim the quilt edges and attach the binding (see page 157).

BLOCK A ASSEMBLY DIAGRAM

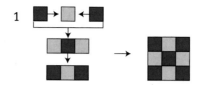

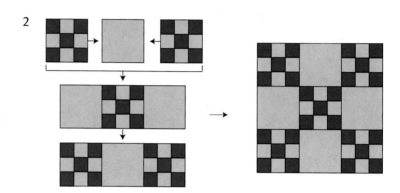

BLOCK B ASSEMBLY DIAGRAM

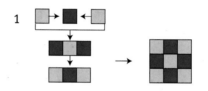

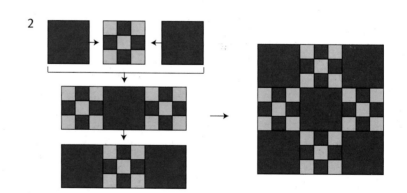

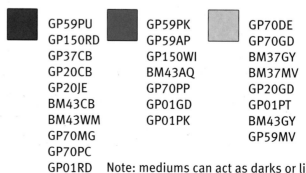

GP59PU	GP59PK	GP70DE
GP150RD	GP59AP	GP70GD
GP37CB	GP150WI	BM37GY
GP20CB	BM43AQ	BM37MV
GP20JE	GP70PP	GP20GD
BM43CB	GP01GD	GP01PT
BM43WM	GP01PK	BM43GY
GP70MG		GP59MV
GP70PC		
GP01RD	Note: mediums can act as darks or lights	

72

QUILT ASSEMBLY DIAGRAM

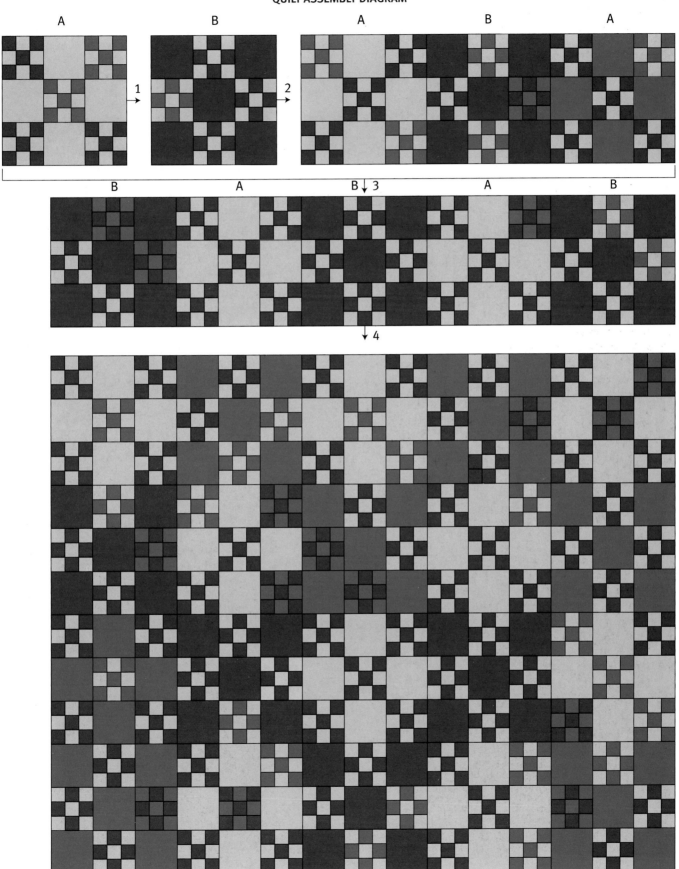

contrast brassica snowballs *

Kaffe Fassett

Time to fussy cut into your floral stash and use some deep, dark black and purple fabrics to sew a batch of these rich Snowball blocks. Five borders of varying widths deliciously frame the floral centre of this quilt.

SIZE OF QUILT
The finished quilt will measure approx. 73in x 78½in (185.5cm x 199.5cm)

MATERIALS
Fabrics calculated at minimum width of fabric of approx. 40in (101.6cm), unless otherwise stated

Patchwork Fabrics
BRASSICA
Dark   PJ51DK   1½yd (1.4m)
(extra allowed for fussy cutting)
Sky   PJ51SK   1½yd (1.4m)
(extra allowed for fussy cutting)
SPOT
Noir   GP70NR   ⅞yd (80cm)
Grape   GP70GP   ⅞yd (80cm)
ZIG ZAG
White   BM43WH   ½yd (45cm)
BUTTON FLOWER
Black   GP152BK   1⅜yd (00cm)
BROCADE PEONY
Grey   PJ62GY   1½yd (00cm)

Backing Fabric
ELEPHANT FLOWER
Purple   BM56PU   5yd (4.5m)
of standard width fabric

Binding
SPOT
Noir   GP70NR   ⅝yd (60cm)

Batting
81in x 86in (206cm x 219cm)

Quilting Thread
Machine quilting thread

PATCH SHAPES
The centre of this quilt is pieced using a Snowball block. This block is traditionally made from an octagon and four triangles, but in this case it is made the easy way with a large square and 4 small squares, using a stitch and flip technique on the four corner squares. The corners are then trimmed and flipped back to replace the corners of the large square.
The large squares are fussy cut from PJ51DK and PJ51SK, with the light and dark flowers alternated to obtain a checkerboard effect.
The quilt centre is surrounded by 5 borders of different widths.

CUTTING OUT
Block large square From PJ51DK fussy cut 21 brassica motifs. From PJ51SK fussy cut 21 brassica motifs. The easiest way to fussy cut the brassicas is to place a 6in (15.2cm) square quilting ruler centrally over each motif and then cut the square.

Block small square Cut 2in (5cm) wide strips across the width of the fabric. Each strip will give 20 patches per fabric width. Cut 168 squares in GP70NR.

Borders
To avoid a quilt with uneven, wavy edges it is advisable to cut the border strips as they are needed, measuring the quilt across the centre horizontally and vertically at each border stage. For Borders 2, 3, 4 and 5 you will need to join sufficient width of fabric strips end to end to achieve the correct lengths.

Border 1 In order that the strips in this border have a horizontal zig zag pattern, cut the strips as follows. Cut 2 strips 3½in (8.9cm) wide across the width of the fabric in BM43WH for the top and bottom borders. Trim each strip to 3½in x 39½in (8.9cm x 100.3cm).
Cut 8 strips down the remaining length of the fabric for the side borders, each 3½in x 11in (8.9cm x 28cm). Join 4 strips end to end and trim to 3½in x 39in (8.9 x 99cm). Repeat with the other 4 strips.

Border 2 Cut 3in (7.6cm) wide strips across the width of the fabric in GP152BK. Cut 2 strips for side borders, each 3in x 45in (7.6cm x 114.3cm), and 2 strips for top and bottom borders, each 3in x 44½in (7.6cm x 113cm).

Border 3 Cut 8½in (21.6cm) wide strips across the width of the fabric in PJ62GY. Cut 2 strips for side borders, each 8½in x 50in (21.6cm x 127cm), and 2 strips for top and bottom borders, each 8½in x 60½in (21.6cm x 153.7cm).

Border 4 Cut 4in (10.2cm) wide strips across the width of the fabric in GP70GP. Cut 2 strips for side borders, each 4in x 66in (10.2cm x 167.6cm), and 2 strips for top and bottom borders, each 4in x 67½in (10.2cm x 171.5cm).

Border 5 Cut 3½in (8.9cm) wide strips across the width of the fabric in GP152BK. Cut 2 strips for side borders, each 3½in x 73in (8.9cm x 185.4cm), and 2 strips for top and bottom borders, each 3½in x 73½in (8.9cm x 186.7cm).

Binding
Cut 8 strips 2½in (6.4cm) wide across the width of the fabric in GP70NR.

Backing
Cut 2 pieces 40½in x 86½in (103cm x 220cm) in BM56PU.

MAKING THE BLOCKS
To make the Snowball blocks take 1 large square and 4 small squares as in the Block Assembly Diagram. On the back of each small square mark a diagonal line. Place 1 small square onto each corner of the large square, right sides together and matching edges and with the marked lines as shown. Sew along the marked

BLOCK ASSEMBLY DIAGRAM

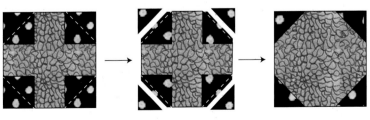

1   2   3

75

lines on each of the 4 small squares (diagram 1). Trim the corners to a ¼in (6mm) seam allowance (diagram 2). Press the corners out (diagram 3). Check the block is 6in (15.2cm) square.
Repeat this process to make 42 blocks in total.

MAKING THE QUILT
Use a ¼in (6mm) seam allowance throughout. Arrange the blocks into 7 rows of 6 blocks, alternating the fabrics as shown in the Quilt Centre Assembly Diagram.
Sew the blocks together into rows. Now sew the rows together, matching seams neatly, to complete the quilt centre.

ADDING THE BORDERS
Refer to the Borders Diagram for assembly details. Use ¼in (6mm) seams throughout and press seams outwards each time. Check the measurement of the quilt each time before adding a border.
Starting with the Border 1 strips, pin the shorter strips to the sides of the quilt, matching the centre point of the border with the centre point of the quilt. Sew into place, easing to fit if need be.
Add the longer strips of Border 1 to the top and bottom of the quilt in the same way.
Continue in this way to add Borders 2, 3, 4 and 5.

FINISHING THE QUILT
Press the quilt top. Seam the backing pieces together using a ¼in (6mm) seam allowance to form a piece approx. 81in x 87in (205.7cm x 221cm).
Layer the quilt top, batting and backing, and baste together (see page 156).
Quilt around the large flowers in the outside borders. Stitch in the ditch on each of the border seams and around each Snowball block. Quilt a zigzag pattern down the centre of the zigzag fabric border. The quilt shown used a variegated quilting thread to tone with the fabrics.
Trim the quilt edges and attach the binding (see page 157).

QUILT CENTRE ASSEMBLY DIAGRAM

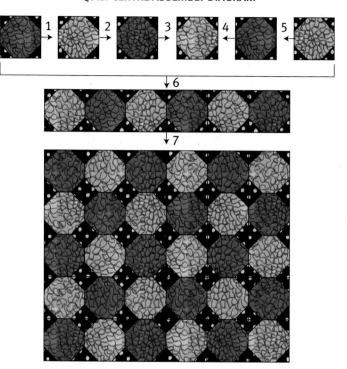

BORDERS DIAGRAM

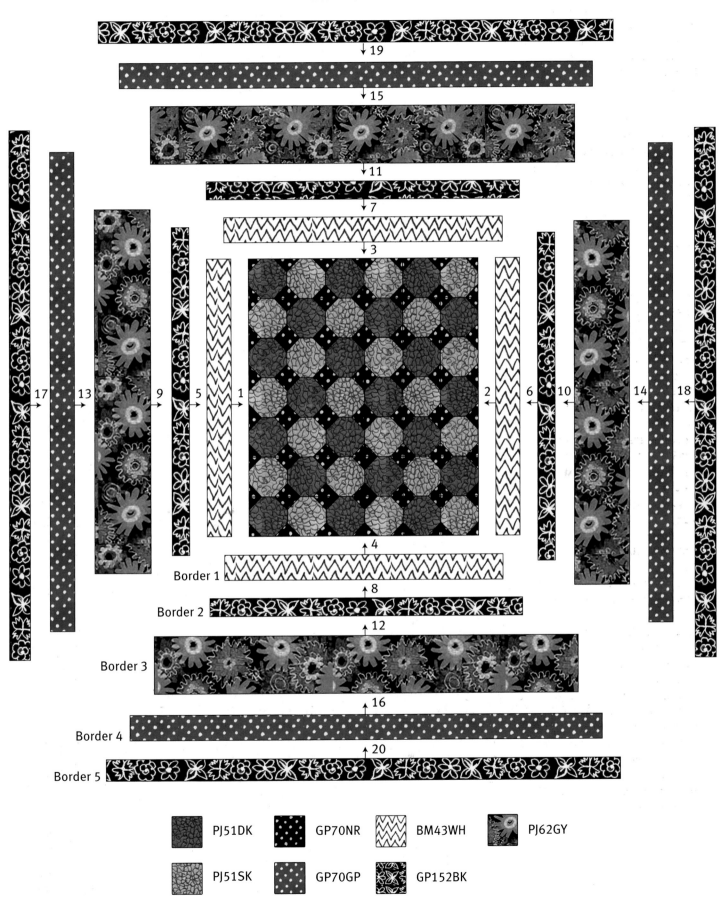

Border 1
Border 2
Border 3
Border 4
Border 5

PJ51DK   GP70NR   BM43WH   PJ62GY

PJ51SK   GP70GP   GP152BK

shadow play **

Kaffe Fassett

This is a scrappy quilt and it is not necessary to place each fabric in exactly the same place as in the original. The blocks are made with one light and one dark fabric for the triangles. The on-point blocks are separated by sashing, with the same fabric used for the border.

SIZE OF QUILT
The finished quilt will measure approx. 73¾in x 73¾in (187cm x 187cm)

MATERIALS
Fabrics calculated at minimum width of fabric of approx. 40in (101.6cm), unless otherwise stated

Patchwork Fabrics
ABORIGINAL DOT
Silver	GP71SV	3yd (2.75m)
Pear	GP71PR	¾yd (70cm)
Chocolate	GP71CL	½yd (45cm)
Pumpkin	GP71PN	¼yd (25cm)
Lilac	GP71LI	¼yd (25cm

SPOT
Shocking	GP70SK	¼yd (25cm)
Lavender	GP70LV	¼yd (25cm)
Lichen	GP70LN	½yd (45cm)
Peach	GP70PH	½yd (45cm)

GUINEA FLOWER
Brown	GP59BR	¼yd (25cm)

PAPERWEIGHT
Pink	GP20PK	¼yd (25cm)

ROMAN GLASS
Pink	GP01PK	¼yd (25cm)

JUPITER
Purple	GP131PU	¼yd (25cm)

JUMBLE
Ochre	BM53OC	¼yd (25cm)

ZIG ZAG
Rare	BM43RR	¼yd (25cm)

WOVEN CATERPILLAR STRIPE
Yellow	WCSYE	¼yd (25cm)

WOVEN NARROW STRIPE
Spice	WNSSI	¼yd (25cm)

Backing Fabric
JUMBLE
Ochre	BM53OC	5yd (4.6m)

of standard width fabric

Binding
ABORIGINAL DOT
Silver	GP71SV	¾yd (70cm)

Batting
82in x 82in (208cm x 208cm)

Quilting Thread
Machine quilting thread

TEMPLATE

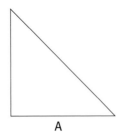

A

PATCH SHAPES
The blocks are assembled from three different patches – 3½in (8.9cm) squares and two sizes of triangles. The larger triangle is created in two different ways – from a 5½in (14cm) square, cut across both diagonals to yield 4 quarter-square triangles; and from a 3⅞in (9.8cm) square cut across one diagonal to yield 2 half-square triangles. These methods ensure that, when sewn, the fabric grainline runs along the outside edge of the triangles.
Use Template A to cut the smaller corner triangles.

CUTTING OUT
Border
Cut the border strips first in GP71SV, cutting 4 lengths 3½in x 68¼in (8.9cm x 173.3cm) (along the length of the fabric).

Sashing
In GP71SV cut 64 rectangles each 3½in x 9½in (8.9cm x 24.1cm).
For the sashing setting triangles, cut 4 squares 5½in x 5½in (14cm x 14cm) in GP71SV. Cut each square diagonally twice, to make 4 quarter-square triangles, for a total of 16 setting triangles.

Tip
If you wish to make different colour combinations in some of the blocks, there is plenty of extra fabric.

For the sashing and border squares cut a total of 28 squares 3½in x 3½in (7.6cm x 7.6cm) in GP71SV.

Blocks
In GP71PR cut 25 squares 3½in x 3½in (7.6cm x 7.6cm) (for centres of whole blocks).
In GP71PR cut 3 squares 5½in x 5½in (14cm x 14cm). Cut diagonally twice, for a total of 12 large triangles (for the half-blocks).
In GP71PR cut 2 squares 3in x 3in (7.6cm x 7.6cm). Cut each square diagonally once, for a total of 4 small triangles (for corner triangles in the quarter-blocks).

Cut the rest of the fabrics into two sizes of triangle, large and small.
For the large triangles, cut a square 3⅞in x 3⅞in (9.8cm x 9.8cm). Cut once diagonally into 2 large triangles. Cut the small triangles using Template A.

From GP71CL cut 24 large squares, to make 48 large triangles. Cut 2 small triangles using Template A.
From GP71PN cut 18 large squares, to make 36 large triangles. Cut 1 small triangle using Template A.
From GP71LI cut 13 large squares, to make 26 large triangles. Cut 1 small triangle using Template A.
From GP70SK cut 6 large squares, to make 12 large triangles. Cut 3 small triangles using Template A.
From GP70LV cut 19 large squares, to make 38 large triangles (you will only use 37 of these). Cut 1 small triangle using Template A.
From GP70LN cut 21 large squares, to make 42 large triangles. Cut 3 small triangles using Template A.
From GP70PH cut 23 large squares, to make 46 large triangles (you will only use 45 of these). Cut 5 small triangles using Template A.
From GP59BR cut 19 large squares, to make 38 large triangles. Cut 4 small triangles using Template A.
From GP20PK cut 20 large squares, to make 40 large triangles.
From GP01PK cut 18 large squares to make 36 large triangles (you will only use 35 of these). Cut 2 small triangles using template A.

From GP131PU cut 18 large squares, to make 36 large triangles (you will only use 35 of these). Cut 2 small triangles using Template A.

From BM53OC cut 18 large squares, to make 36 large triangles (you will only use 35 of these). Cut 2 small triangles using Template A.

From BM43RR cut 18 large squares, to make 36 large triangles (you will only use 35 of these). Cut 2 small triangles using Template A.

From WCSYE cut 10 large squares, to make 20 large triangles (you will only use 19 of these).

From WNSSI cut 7 large squares, to make 14 large triangles. Cut 4 small triangles using Template A.

Binding
In BP70SV cut 8 strips 2½in (6.4cm) wide across the width.

Backing
In BM53OC, cut 2 lengths approximately 40in x 84in (101.6cm x 213.3cm).

MAKING THE BLOCKS
There are 25 whole blocks, 3 half-blocks for the top, 3 half-blocks for the bottom, 6 half-blocks for the sides, 4 different quarter-blocks for the corners. Note: in all blocks the darker triangles point down and the lighter triangles point up.

For the whole blocks Choose 8 large triangles of a lighter fabric and 8 large triangles of a darker fabric, and 1 GP71PR square. Sew a pair of light and dark triangles together along the longest side of the triangle to make a two-toned square. Make 8 of these. Following the Full Block Assembly Diagram, sew the 8 two-toned squares and one solid square into a nine-patch block.

For the 3 bottom half-blocks For each half-block you will need 5 light triangles, 3 dark triangles and a large GP71PR triangle.

For the 3 top half-blocks For each half-block you will need 5 dark large triangles, 3 light ones and a large GP71PR triangle. Each half-block has 3 two-toned squares. When making these half-blocks, refer to the Half-Block Assembly Diagram and the quilt photo and follow carefully for the placement of the darks and lights and the small and large triangles.

FULL BLOCK ASSEMBLY DIAGRAM

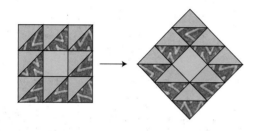

HALF-BLOCK ASSEMBLY DIAGRAM

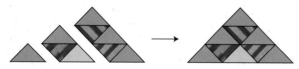

HALF-BLOCK ASSEMBLY DIAGRAM (SIDE)

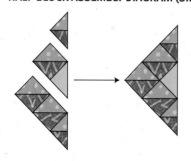

CORNER QUARTER-BLOCK ASSEMBLY DIAGRAM

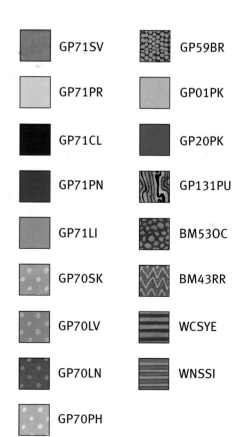

GP71SV	GP59BR
GP71PR	GP01PK
GP71CL	GP20PK
GP71PN	GP131PU
GP71LI	BM53OC
GP70SK	BM43RR
GP70LV	WCSYE
GP70LN	WNSSI
GP70PH	

For the side half-blocks Choose 3 large and 2 small dark triangles, 3 large and 2 small light triangles and one large GP71PR triangle. Each half-block has 3 two-toned squares. Note: the left side and the right side triangles are not the same. For assembly, follow the Half-Block Assembly Diagram (Side) and the quilt photo carefully.

Corners Each corner of the quilt is different. Each quarter-block has 1 two-toned block, 1 light (or dark) large triangle, 1 light and one dark small triangle and 1 small GP71PR triangle. Follow the Corner Quarter-Block Assembly Diagram to select the pieces and then make each of the 4 corners.

ASSEMBLING THE QUILT
Lay out the whole and partial blocks in diagonal rows, as in the Quilt Assesmbly Diagram. Sew a sashing rectangle between each block/partial block, as shown.

Sew those blocks with sashings into diagonal rows following the diagram. The rest of the sashing rectangles are sewn into long strips using the squares to connect them and with large triangles at each end. Follow the diagram to assemble each long sashing strip. Alternating blocks and sashing strips, sew the long diagonal rows together. Add the border by sewing a long border strip to the left side and then to the right side of the quilt. Sew a 3½in (8.9cm) square of GP71SV to both ends of the remaining border strips and then sew these to the top and bottom of the quilt.

FINISHING THE QUILT
Press the quilt top. Seam the backing pieces using a ¼in (6mm) seam allowance to form a piece approximately 82in x 82in (208cm x 208cm).
Layer the quilt top, batting and backing, and baste together (see page 156).
The quilt shown was long-arm quilted in an all-over pattern.
Trim the quilt edges and attach the binding (see page 157).

ripples **

Kaffe Fassett

This is a traditional design using half-square triangles to frame a square made from two triangles. There are 50 blocks in the quilt set on point, with half-blocks for side setting triangles and quarter-blocks for corner triangles. Careful piecing using a quick method will help you create this stunning quilt. The contrast of light and dark fabrics for the triangles making up each block creates the distinctive Lady of the Lake block.

SIZE OF QUILT
The finished quilt will measure approx. 70¼in x 83½in (178.5cm x 212cm).

MATERIALS
Fabrics calculated at minimum width of fabric of approx. 40in (101.6cm), unless otherwise stated

Patchwork Fabrics
JUMBLE
Lemon	BM53LM	¼yd (25cm)
Turquoise	BM53TQ	¾yd (70cm)
Moss	BM53MS	¾yd (70cm)

BIG BLOOMS
| Duck Egg | GP91DE | ¼yd (25cm) |

PAPERWEIGHT
| Algae | GP20AL | ⅝yd (60cm) |

JAPANESE CHRYSANTHEMUM
| Spring | PJ41SP | ¼yd (25cm) |

VINE
| Gold | GP151GD | ¼yd (25cm) |

ROMAN GLASS
| Leaf | GP01LF | ½yd (45cm) |

ZIG ZAG
Aqua	BM43AQ	⅞yd (80cm)
Yellow	BM43YE	¼yd (25cm)
Multi	BM43MU	¾yd (70cm)

JUPITER
| Malachite | GP131MA | ⅝yd (60cm) |

BUTTON FLOWERS
| Aqua | GP152AQ | ¼yd (25cm) |
| Pink | GP152PK | ¼yd (25cm) |

ABORIGINAL DOT
| Mint | GP71MT | 3½yd (3.25m) |

STRATA
| Spring | GP150SP | ⅝yd (60cm) |

MILLEFIORE
| Jade | GP92JA | ⅞yd (80cm) |

LAKE BLOSSOMS
| Pink | GP93PK | ¼yd (25cm) |
| Yellow | GP93YE | ¼yd (25cm) |

Backing Fabric
CIRCLES
| Pastel | QBGP02PT | 2¼yd (2m) of |

108in (274cm) wide

Binding
ZIG ZAG
| Aqua | BM43AQ | ⅝yd (60cm) |

Batting
78in x 93in (198cm x 236cm)

Quilting Thread
Machine quilting thread

TEMPLATES

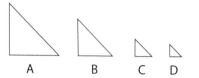

A   B   C   D

PATCH SHAPES
The Lady of the Lake block in this quilt finishes at 10in (25.4cm) and is made using 2 triangle patch shapes (Templates A and C). The blocks are set on point, with the light triangle always on top. The blocks are then stitched into diagonal rows. The side edges and the corners of the quilt are filled in using half-blocks and quarter-blocks. These use the A and C triangle shapes and 2 additional triangle shapes (Templates B and D).

CUTTING OUT
Template A Cut 6⅞in (17.5cm) wide strips across the width of the fabric. Each strip will give 10 patches per fabric width. Cut into 6⅞in (17.5cm) squares and then cut each square once diagonally to make 2 triangles.
You will need the following numbers of triangles (Template A):
10 in PJ41SP and BM43AQ, 9 in GP92JA, 7 in GP152AQ, BM53TQ and BM43MU, 6 in BM53MS, GP152PK, GP91DE and BM53LM, 5 in BM43YE, GP93PK and GP93YE, 4 in GP20AL, GP150SP, GP131MA and GP151GD, 3 in GP01LF.

Template B Using the leftover strips from Template A, trim them to 5⅛in (13cm) wide. Cut into 5⅛in (13cm) squares and then cut each square in half once diagonally to make 2 triangles, using Template B as a guide.

You will need the following numbers of triangles (Template B):
3 in GP131MA, GP151GD and BM53MS, 2 in GP150SP, GP91DE and GP152PK, 1 in PJ41SP, GP93PK, BM53TQ, GP20AL, BM43MU, GP152AQ, GP92JA, BM43YE and BM53LM.

Template C Use the quick piecing method for the template C triangles. These half-square triangle units are created from 6in squares – see Half-square Triangle Diagram. Cut 6in (15.2cm) wide strips across the width of the fabric. Each strip will give you 6 squares per fabric width. Cut the following squares (these will give spare half-square triangles):
122 in GP71MT, 19 in BM43AQ and GP92JA, 15 in BM53TQ, BM53MS and BM43MU, 12 in GP131MA, 11 in GP20AL, 10 in GP150SP, 6 in GP01LF.

Template D Using the leftover fabric, cut a 2¼in (5.7cm) wide strip in GP71MT, cut into 12 squares, then cut each square once diagonally to make 24 triangles. Using template D and checking the grain line, cut another 24 triangles in the following fabrics:
6 in BM53MS and GP131MA, 3 in GP150SP, 2 in BM53TQ, GP20AL, BM43AQ and BM53MU, 1 in GP92JA.

Binding
Cut 8 strips 2½in (6.4cm) wide across the width of the fabric in BM43AQ.

Backing
From extra wide 108in (274cm) backing fabric, cut a piece 78in x 93in (198cm x 236cm) in QBGP02PT.

MAKING THE BLOCKS
To make the centre of a block sew a dark and a light 6⅞in (17.5cm) triangle together to make a 6½in (16.5in) unit. The half-square triangles surrounding each block centre are made using a quick piecing method (see Half-square Triangle Diagram). Each 6in (15.2cm) square will give 8 half-square triangle units. You need 16 half-square triangles per full block. The half-blocks (sides) need 7 half-square triangle units, and the corners need 3. Using a design wall and following the Block Assembly Diagrams will help with the placement of the finished blocks.

Quick pieced half-square triangles

Place a 6in (15.2cm) square of GP71MT right sides together with a print square and draw two diagonal lines from corner to corner (see Half-square Triangle Diagram). Stitch ¼in (6mm) either side of the diagonal lines. Cut along the marked diagonal lines and also the vertical and horizontal lines, marked with arrows on the diagram. Press the half-square triangle units and trim each one to 2½in (6.4cm) square.

Repeat with all the GP71MT and print squares. Note: there will be many half-square triangle units left over.

Full block assembly

To assemble a full block, use a ¼in (6mm) seam allowance throughout and follow the sequence shown in the Full Block Assembly Diagram. Follow the Quilt Assembly Diagram to piece 50 blocks in total.

Side half-block assembly

The top and bottom of the quilt are filled in with horizontal half-blocks, pieced in the same way as the main blocks (see the Side Half-Block Assembly Diagram). Take care that the pale GP71MT background triangles are in the correct positions. The sides of the quilt are filled in by making vertical half-blocks, which use additional Template shapes B and D. The blocks are reversed on the opposite side of the quilt.

Corner quarter-blocks assembly

Four quarter-blocks are needed to complete the quilt corners. Each quarter block is pieced differently, so refer to the Corner Quarter-blocks Assembly Diagram.

MAKING THE QUILT

Following the Quilt Assembly Diagram, lay out all the full blocks in diagonal rows, with the half-blocks along the sides and the quarter-blocks in the corners. Sew the blocks together into diagonal rows, adding half-blocks to the end of each row. Sew the rows together and then sew the corner quarter-blocks in place to complete the quilt centre.

HALF-SQUARE TRIANGLE DIAGRAM

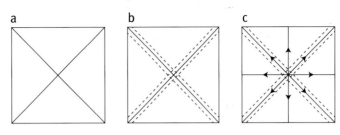

FULL BLOCK ASSEMBLY DIAGRAM

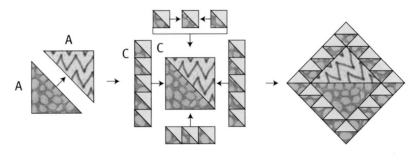

SIDE HALF-BLOCK ASSEMBLY DIAGRAM

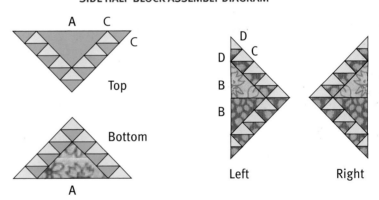

CORNER QUARTER-BLOCKS ASSEMBLY DIAGRAM

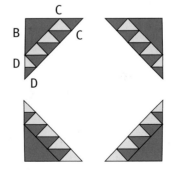

FINISHING THE QUILT

Press the quilt top and the 78in x 93in (198cm x 236cm) piece of backing fabric. Layer the quilt top, batting and backing, and baste together (see page 156). Using machine quilting thread, quilt in the ditch along the diagonal seams and around the on-point squares.

Trim the quilt edges and attach the binding to the quilt (see page 157).

Tip
You could use the leftover half-square triangles and fabric to make up a cushion cover to match your quilt.

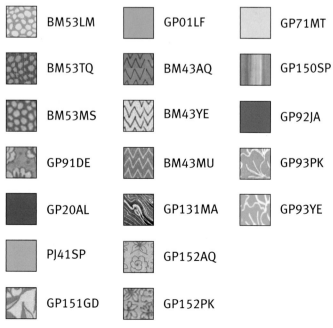

BM53LM	GP01LF	GP71MT
BM53TQ	BM43AQ	GP150SP
BM53MS	BM43YE	GP92JA
GP91DE	BM43MU	GP93PK
GP20AL	GP131MA	GP93YE
PJ41SP	GP152AQ	
GP151GD	GP152PK	

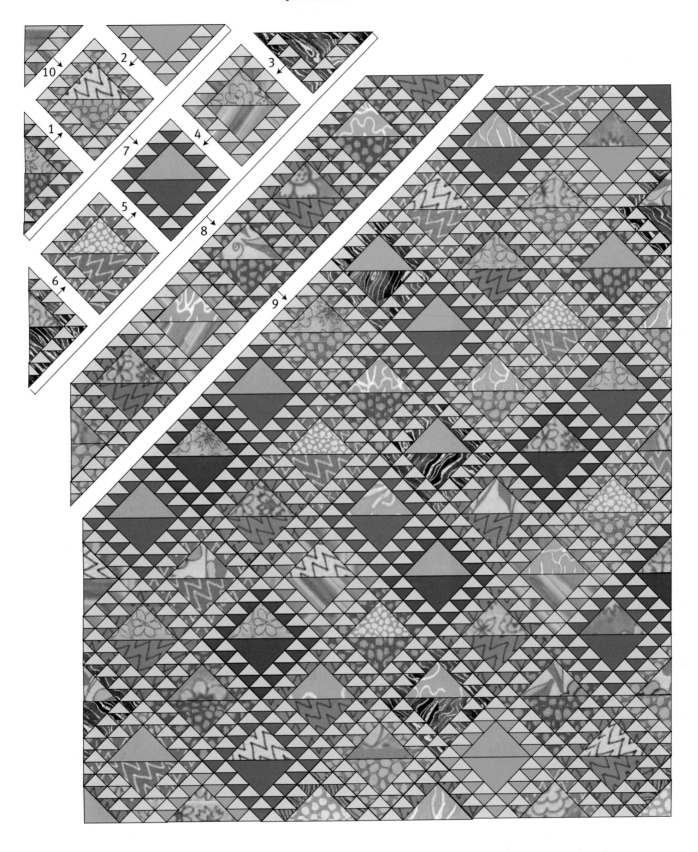

dancing blocks ***

Kaffe Fassett

This is a first-class challenge for the expert quilter and success depends on a good inset seam technique. The quilt centre is created with two shapes, a square and a diamond, with the squares fussy cut to feature a flower motif. The shapes are pieced in rows that slant to the left and right alternately. Three additional triangle shapes are used for setting and corner triangles. There is liveliness in the 2D motion of the blocks, but also a 3D character that our eyes crave to find.

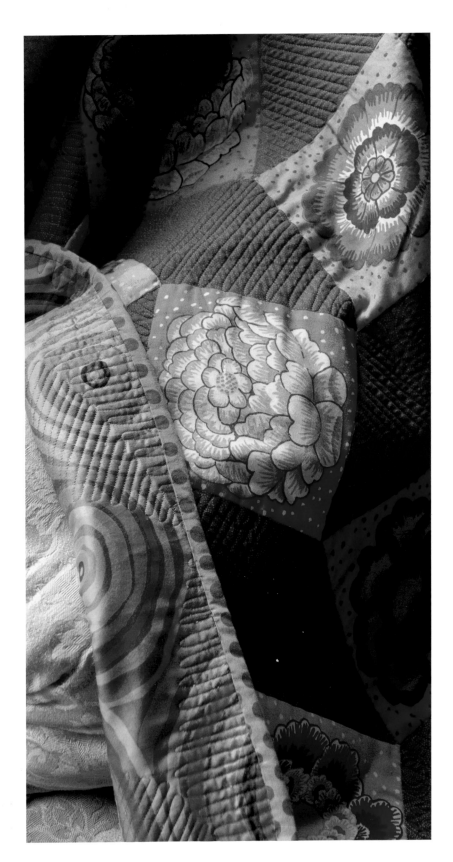

SIZE OF QUILT
The finished quilt will measure approx.
80in x 96in (203cm x 244cm)

MATERIALS
Fabrics calculated at minimum width of fabric of approx. 40in (101.6cm), unless otherwise stated

Patchwork Fabrics
ABORIGINAL DOTS
Plum	GP71PL	3¾yd (3.5m)

CORSAGE
Gold	GP149GD	1¼yd (1.2m)
Scarlet	GP149SC	1¼yd (1.2m)
Orange	GP149OR	1¼yd (1.2m)
Blue	GP149BL	1¼yd (1.2m)

Backing Fabric
CIRCLES
Green   QBGP02GN   2½yd (2.3m) of 108in (274cm) wide

Binding
SPOT
Orange   GP70OR   ¾yd (70cm)

Batting
88in x 104in (224cm x 264cm)

Quilting Thread
Machine quilting thread

TEMPLATES

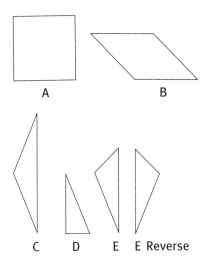

PATCH SHAPES

The quilt is made up of square patch shapes (Template A) fussy cut from the flowers of the four Corsage fabrics, and diamond patch shapes (Template B) which serve as background for the flower blocks. Triangle patch shapes are used to fill in around the edges (Template C) and on the corners (Template D, E and E reverse) of the quilt.

CUTTING OUT

Template A
Cut 6½in (16.5cm) strips across the width of the fabric making sure that the row of flowers is centred. Each strip will give you 6 flower patches. You need 119 squares in total.
Cut 30 in GP149GD, 30 in GP149SC, 30 in GP149BL and 29 in GP149OR.

Template B
Cut 4⅝in (11.7cm) strips across the width of the fabric. Each strip will give you 5 diamond shapes. Cut 119 in GP71PL.

Template C
Cut 3in (7.6cm) wide strips across the width of the fabric. Each strip will give 4 triangles per fabric width, if the template is rotated alternately along the strip. Cut a total of 29 triangles in GP71PL. These setting triangles are used to fill in around the edges of the quilt.

Template D
Use the fabric left over from cutting the Template B and C shapes (checking the grain line with the template). Cut 2 triangles using Template D in GP71PL for the top left and bottom left side of the quilt.

Template E
Use the fabric left over from cutting the Template B and C shapes (make sure you check the grain line with the template). In GP71PL cut 1 triangle using Template E and 1 triangle using Template E Reverse, for the top right and side of the quilt.

Binding
Cut 10 strips 2½in (6.4cm) wide across the width of the fabric in GP70OR.

Backing
From extra wide backing, cut a piece 88in (224cm) long x 104in (224cm) wide in QBGP02GN.

MAKING THE QUILT

Refer to the Quilt Assembly Diagram for the fabric sequence and the orientation of each row. Laying out each row in turn will help to keep the fabric sequence correct. You could vary the positions of the squares if you prefer.
Using a ¼in (6mm) seam allowance throughout, join the squares (A) and diamonds (B) into 17 rows using an inset seam technique (see page 64 for general principles). The A and B rows will have a stepped appearance when joined but will be tilted when the remaining shapes are added. Press seams open.
Now join the rows together, still using inset seams. Press seams open.
Once all the rows are joined, fill in the edges of the quilt with Template C setting triangles, again using inset seams.
Add 2 Template D triangles – one to the top left and one to the bottom left corner. Finally, add a Template E triangle to the top right end of the quilt, and a Template E Reverse triangle on the top right side, as shown in the Quilt Assembly Diagram. You may find it easier to sew these two triangles in one unit before adding it to the top right corner of the quilt with inset seams as before.

FINISHING THE QUILT

Press the quilt top and the backing fabric piece.
Layer the quilt top, batting and backing, and baste together (see page 156).
Quilt using a tonal thread. This is not a quilt for beginners due to all the inset seams. In order to keep the quilt square you may need to ease in some of areas of the fabric (see also the Tip). If you are quilting it on a domestic machine make sure that you baste it well and closer than normal, about every 2in (5cm) instead of the usual 4in–5in (10cm–12.5cm).
Trim the quilt edges and attach the binding (see page 157).

Tip
You might find it useful to add a border to this quilt, to help stabilize the edges for quilting. The border could be temporary or permanent. Remember though that adding a border will alter the fabric requirements for the backing, batting and binding.

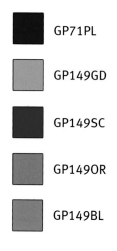

GP71PL

GP149GD

GP149SC

GP149OR

GP149BL

QUILT ASSEMBLY DIAGRAM

floral plaid **

Kaffe Fassett

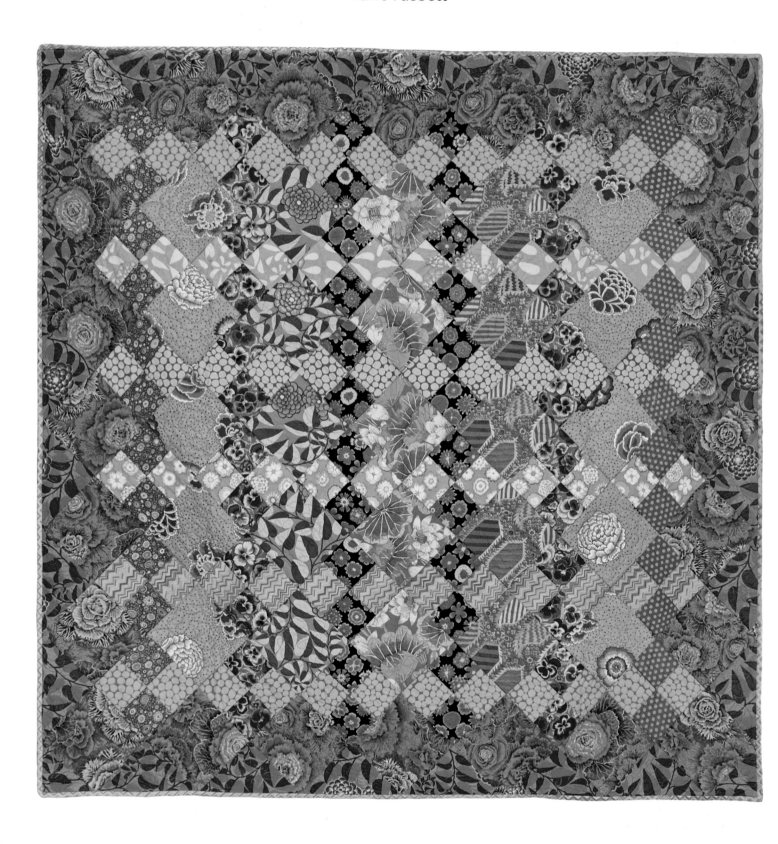

This quilt is a delight to make. It uses carefully chosen fabrics to give the illusion of diamonds 'on point' vertically within the quilt. The quilt is joined together in diagonal rows, making it easy to add the setting and corner triangles, which make up the frame around the outside of the quilt.

SIZE OF QUILT
The finished quilt will measure approx. 79in x 79in (200.5cm x 200.5cm)

MATERIALS
Fabrics calculated at minimum width of fabric of approx. 40in (101.6cm), unless otherwise stated

Patchwork Fabrics
VINE
Emerald	GP151EM	½yd (45cm)
Purple	GP151PU	1yd (1m)
Grey	GP151GY	¼yd (25cm)

BRASSICA
Rust	PJ51RU	1½yd (1.5m)

STRIPED HERALDIC
Turquoise	GP153TQ	½yd (45cm)

CORSAGE
Pink	GP149PK	¾yd (70cm)

LAKE BLOSSOMS
Magenta	GP93MG	½yd (45cm)

PANSIES
Orange	PJ76OR	⅜yd (35cm)

BUTTON FLOWERS
Black	GP152BK	⅜yd (35cm)
Grey	GP152GY	¼yd (25cm)

JUMBLE
Moss	BM53MS	⅜yd (35cm)
Turquoise	BM53TQ	¼yd (25cm)

ZIG ZAG
Aqua	BM43AQ	¼yd (25cm)

SPOT
Fuchsia	GP701FU	¼yd (25cm)

ROMAN GLASS
Red	GP01RD	¼yd (25cm)

Backing Fabric
BUTTON FLOWERS
Black	GP152BK	5½yd (5m) of standard width fabric

Batting
87in x 87in (221cm x 221cm)

Binding
ZIG ZAG
Aqua	BM43AQ	⅝yd (60cm)

Quilting Thread
Machine quilting thread

TEMPLATES

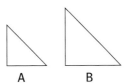

A   B

PATCH SHAPES
The quilt centre is made up of 4½in (11.4cm) square patches pieced into four-patch blocks. These are alternated with un-pieced 8½in (21.6cm) squares. The blocks and squares are set on point with large setting triangles (Template A) to fill in along the quilt sides. Template A is given as a half template on page 000, so see instructions there for preparing this template. The corners of the quilt are filled with smaller triangle shapes (Template B).

CUTTING OUT
Four-patch squares Cut 4½in (11.4cm) wide strips across the width of the fabric. Each strip will give you 8 squares 4½in (11.4cm) per fabric width.
Cut 24 in BM53MS, 24 in PJ76OR, 24 in GP152BK, 12 in BM53TQ, 12 in GP01RD, 12 in GP152GY, 12 in GP701FU, 12 in BM43AQ and 12 in GP151GY.

Plain squares Cut 8½in (21.6cm) strips across the width of the fabric. Each strip will give you 4 squares 8½in (21.6cm) per fabric width.
Cut 24 in PJ51RU, 10 in GP149PK, 5 in GP153TQ, 5 in GP93MG, 5 in GP151EM.

Template A Cut 3 strips 9¼in (23.5cm) wide across the width of the fabric in GP151PU. Cut each strip into 4 squares 9¼in (23.5cm). Cut each square in half once along the diagonal, using Template A as a guide, to make a total of 24 setting triangles.

Template B Cut 2 squares 6½in (16.5cm) in GP151PU. Cut each square in half once diagonally to make a total of 4 corner triangles.

Backing
In GP152BK cut 2 pieces 40in x 87in (101.6cm x 221cm) and 3 pieces 7½in x 40in (19cm x 101.6cm).

Binding
Cut 8 strips 2½in (6.4cm) wide across the width of the fabric in BM43AQ.

MAKING THE FOUR-PATCH BLOCKS
Using the Quilt Assembly Diagram overleaf as a guide to fabric combinations and a ¼in (6mm) seam allowance throughout, use the 4½in (11.4cm) squares to make 36 four-patch blocks. See the Four-patch Block Assembly Diagram.

MAKING THE QUILT
Take the 36 four-patch blocks and the 49 plain 8½in (21.6cm) squares and referring to the Quilt Assembly Diagram for the fabric sequence, lay out each diagonal row in turn; this will help to keep the fabric sequence correct. (The use of a design wall will help with placement.) Sew the blocks together into 13 diagonal rows, adding the Template A setting triangles to the end of each row. Sew the rows together and then sew the Template B corner triangles in place to complete the quilt centre.

FOUR-PATCH BLOCK ASSEMBLY DIAGRAM

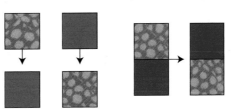

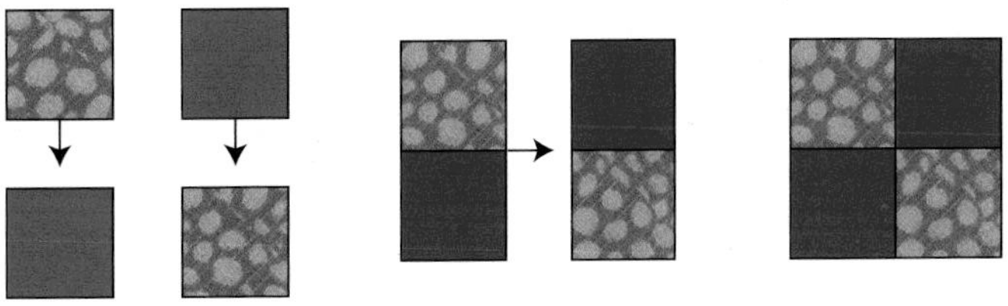

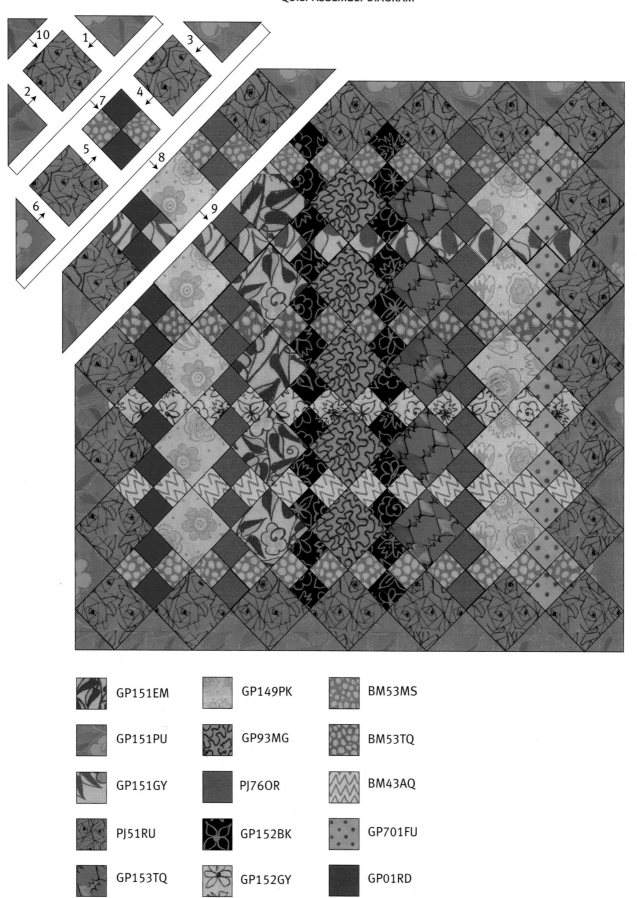

GP151EM	GP149PK	BM53MS
GP151PU	GP93MG	BM53TQ
GP151GY	PJ76OR	BM43AQ
PJ51RU	GP152BK	GP701FU
GP153TQ	GP152GY	GP01RD

FINISHING THE QUILT

Press the quilt top.

Using a ¼in (6mm) seam allowance, sew the narrow backing pieces together end to end and trim to 87in (221cm). Sew an 87in x 40in (221cm x 101.6cm) backing piece to either side of the pieced strip, to form a backing approximately 87in x 87in (221cm x 221cm).

Layer the quilt top, batting and backing, and baste together (see page 156). Quilt in the ditch around the blocks. Stitch large curly spirals on the large squares and smaller curly spirals on the border triangles.

Trim the quilt edges and attach the binding (see page 157).

road to ireland *

Judy Baldwin

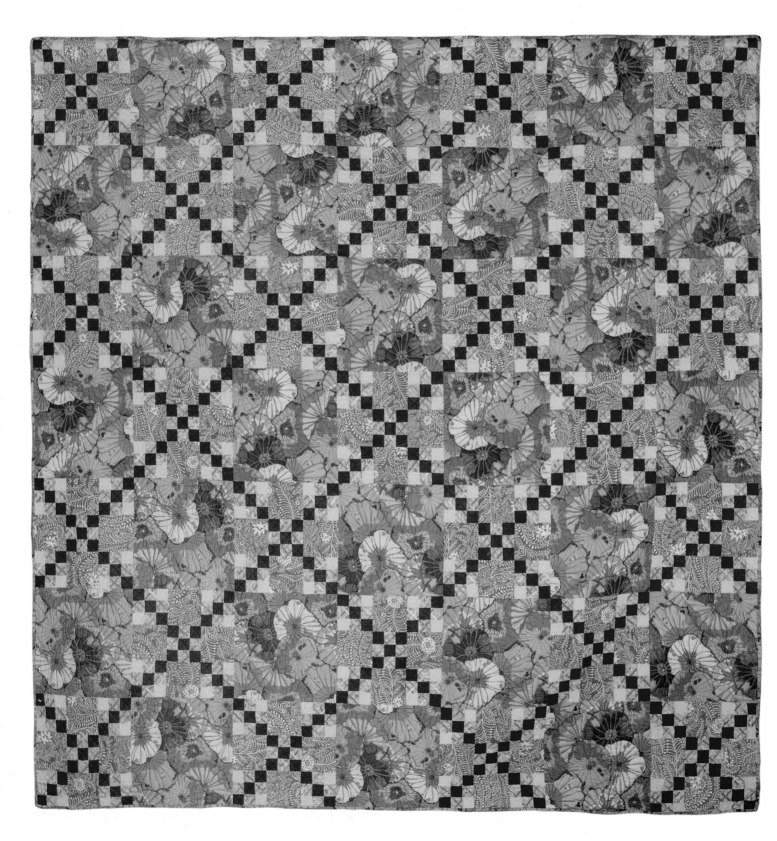

This square quilt is based on a traditional quilt design known as Irish Chain. It is composed of two blocks, one pieced with smaller squares and the other a large unpieced print. The pieced block is a large 9-patch block composed of smaller 9-patch blocks and a coordinating print.

SIZE OF QUILT
The finished quilt will measure approx. 94½ x 94½in (240 x 240cm)

MATERIALS
Fabrics calculated at minimum width of fabric of approx. 40in (101.6cm), unless otherwise stated

Patchwork fabrics
LOTUS
Purple   GP29PU   4¾yd (4.6m)
(includes binding)
FERNS
Purple   GP147PU   2yd (1.8m)
MAD PLAID
Turquoise   BM37TQ   1⅝yd (1.5m)
SHOT COTTON
Bordeaux   SC54   1½yd (1.4m)
Lime   SC43   ¾yd (70cm)

Backing fabric
CIRCLES
Green   QBGP02GN   3yd (2.7m)
of 108in (274cm) wide

Binding
Use spare fabric from LOTUS Purple GP29PU

Batting
103in x 103in (261cm x 261cm)

Quilting Thread
Machine quilting thread

PATCHES
Three different sizes of square patch are used in this quilt. Cut sizes are 2in x 2in (5cm x 5cm), 5in x 5in (12.7cm x 12.7cm) and 14in x 14in (35.5cm x 35.5cm).

CUTTING OUT
Blocks
Using SC54, cut 22 strips 2in (5cm) across the width of the fabric. Cut these strips into 20 squares 2in (5cm). You will need 425 squares.

Using BM37TQ, cut 25 strips 2in (5cm) across the width of the fabric. Cut each strip into 20 squares 2in (5cm). You will need 500 squares.

Using SC43, cut 10 strips 2in (5cm) across the width of the fabric. Cut each strip into 20 squares 2in (5cm). You will need 200 squares.

Using GP147PU, cut 13 strips 5in (12.7cm) across the width of the fabric. Cut each strip into 8 squares 5in (12.7cm). You will need 100 squares.

Using GP29PU, cut 2 strips 14in (35.5cm) wide from the *length* of the fabric. Cut each strip into 14in (35.5cm) squares. You will get 12 squares per strip. You need 24 squares. Reserve the leftover fabric for the binding.

Backing
From the extra-wide QBGP02GN fabric, cut one piece 103in x 103in (261cm x 261cm).

Binding
From GP29PU, cut 3 strips 2½in (6.4cm) x *length* of fabric.

MAKING THE BLOCKS
Using the 2in (5cm) squares cut from SC54, BM37TQ and SC43, create a 9-patch block as shown in the Block 1 Assembly Diagram. Make 100 blocks.

Using the 2in (5cm) squares cut from SC54 and BM37TQ, create a 9-patch block, as shown in the Block 2 Assembly Diagram. Make 25 blocks.

Using the 5in (12.7cm) squares cut from GP147PU and the 9-patch Blocks 1 and 2 previously constructed, piece a large 9-patch block, as shown in the Block 3 Assembly Diagram. Make 25 blocks. These large blocks should measure 14in x 14in (35.5cm x 35.5cm) unfinished.

ASSEMBLING THE QUILT
Follow the Quilt Assembly Diagram carefully to lay out the large 9-patch blocks and the plain squares of GP29PU in 7 rows, each with 7 blocks/squares, alternating the pieced blocks and the plain squares as shown. Using ¼in (6mm) seams, sew each row together. Now sew the rows together.

FINISHING THE QUILT
Press the quilt top and the piece of backing fabric. Layer the quilt top, batting and backing, and baste together (see page 156).
Using machine quilting thread, quilt as desired.
Trim the quilt edges. Sew the 3 binding strips together and trim to a length of about 400in (1016cm). Attach the binding to the quilt (see page 157).

BLOCK 1 ASSEMBLY DIAGRAM

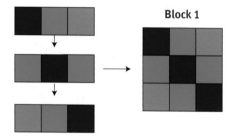

Block 1

BLOCK 2 ASSEMBLY DIAGRAM

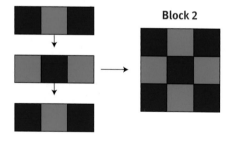

Block 2

BLOCK 3 ASSEMBLY DIAGRAM

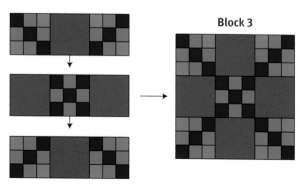

Block 3

QUILT ASSEMBLY DIAGRAM

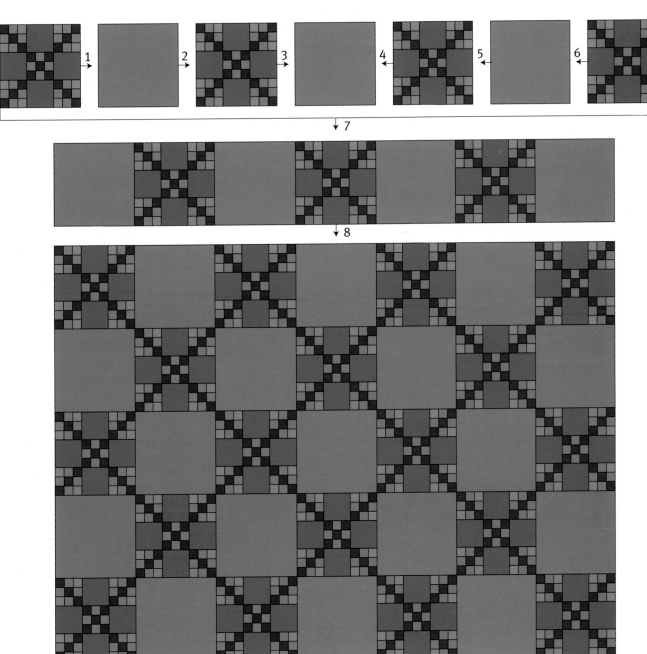

GP29PU

GP147PU

BM37TQ

SC54

SC43

maple leaf medallion **

Liza Prior Lucy

My favourite quilts are medallions. They are never boring to make because each frame around the centre medallion is different. This quilt has a centre chequerboard of squares on point, framed by large triangles. Four borders surround this, two pieced and two plain.

SIZE OF QUILT
The finished quilt will measure approx. 96in x 96in (244cm x 244cm)

MATERIALS
Fabrics calculated at minimum width of fabric of approx. 40in (101.6cm), unless otherwise stated

Patchwork Fabrics
DAHLIA BLOOMS
Succulent   GP54SC   2¾yd (2.5m)
(includes binding)
CORSAGE
Lavender   GP149LV   2yd (1.9m)
MAPLE STREAM
Mauve   PJ80MV   2yd (1.8m)
(extra allowed for fussy cutting)
PAPER FANS
Vintage   GP143VN   1½yd (1.4m)
ABORIGINAL DOT
Wisteria   GP71WS   1¼yd (1.2m)
STRATA
Spring   GP150SP   1yd (90cm)
PAPERWEIGHT
Sludge   GP20SL   ¾yd (70cm)

¼yd (25cm) of each of following:
SPOT
Periwinkle   GP70PE
Apple   GP70AL
ABORIGINAL DOT
Ochre   GP71OC

⅛yd (15cm) each of the following:
SPOT
Taupe   GP70TA
Duck egg   GP70DE
Pond   GP70PO
Grape   GP70GP
Lavender   GP70LV
ABORIGINAL DOT
Ocean   GP71ON
PAPERWEIGHT
Blue   GP20BL

Backing Fabric
CIRCLES
Pastel   QBGP02PT   3yd (2.75m)
of 108in (274in) wide

Binding
DAHLIA BLOOMS
Succulent   GP54SC (use fabric left over after cutting Border 4)

Batting
104in x 104in (264cm x 264cm)

Quilting Thread
Machine quilting thread

TEMPLATES

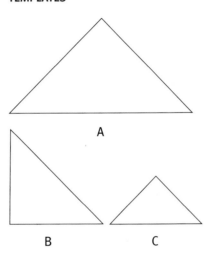

CUTTING OUT
Centre Medallion
For the on-point centre Cut squares 2½in x 2½in (5cm x 5cm) in the following quantities (289 squares in total): 144 in GP20SL, 27 in GP70AL, 18 in GP70PE, 18 in GP71OC, 14 in GP71WS, 14 in GP70LV, 11 in GP70TA, 11 in GP20BL, 9 in GP70DE, 9 in GP70PO, 7 in GP71ON and 7 in GP70GP.

For the large triangles From PJ80MV, cut two squares each 24⅞in x 24⅞in (63.2cm x 63.2cm). Cut each square once diagonally from corner to corner, making 4 triangles in total.

Border 1
Using GP149LV and template A, fussy cut 12 single blossoms. (Note: it may not be possible to completely contain a flower within each triangle, which is fine.) There is enough yardage to select different blossoms, so pick your favourites.

Using template B, fussy cut 8 triangles with no blossoms.
Using GP150SP, cut 4 strips selvedge to selvedge 6⅝in (16.8cm) wide, so the stripes run parallel to the length. Using template A, cut 16 triangles with the base of the triangle parallel to the stripes. Using GP150SP cut 4 squares each 6⅞in x 6⅞in (17.5cm x 17.5cm) and cut two squares diagonally from top right to lower left, and two squares from top left to lower right, for 8 half-square triangles.

Border 2
Using GP143VN, cut 7 strips 6½in (16.5cm) wide from selvedge to selvedge. Remove selvedges and sew together end to end. Cut 2 lengths 72½in (184.1cm) and 2 lengths 60½in (153.7cm).

Border 3
Using PJ80MV, cut 52 squares each 4¾in x 4¾in (12cm x 12cm).
Using GP71WS cut 10 strips each 3⅝in (9.2cm) wide from selvedge to selvedge. Using template C, place the long side of the template parallel to the long edge and flip back and forth to cut 9 triangles from each strip. Cut a total of 88 triangles.
Using GP71WS, cut 16 squares 3⅞in x 3⅞in (9.8cm x 9.8cm) and cut each square once diagonally from corner to corner for 32 half-square triangles.

Border 4
Using GP54SC and cutting along the length of the fabric, cut 2 lengths 6½in x 84½in (16.5cm x 214.6cm) and 2 lengths 6½in x 96½in (16.5cm x 245cm). You may prefer to cut these after you have pieced the quilt, in case your border measurements differ.

Backing
From QBGP02PT cut one piece 104in x 104in (264cm x 264cm).

Binding
From GP54SC (left over from Border 4) cut 4 strips each 2½in (6.4cm) wide x length of fabric. Sew the strips together end to end.

CENTRE CHEQUERBOARD DIAGRAM

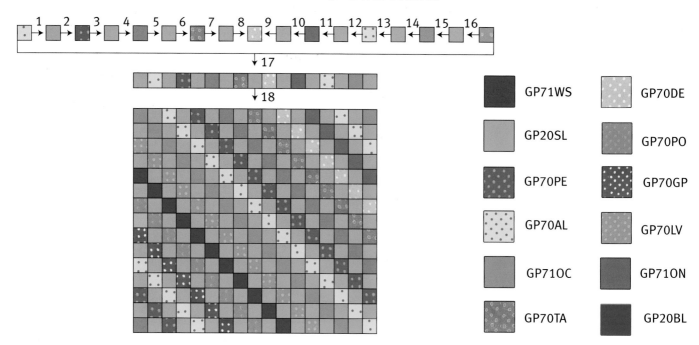

GP71WS	GP70DE
GP20SL	GP70PO
GP70PE	GP70GP
GP70AL	GP70LV
GP71OC	GP71ON
GP70TA	GP20BL

BORDER 1 DIAGRAM

BORDER 3 DIAGRAM

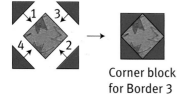

Corner block
for Border 3

MAKING THE QUILT

Use a ¼in (6mm) seam allowance throughout and refer to the Quilt Assembly Diagram as needed.

To make the central medallion chequerboard, follow the Centre Chequerboard Diagram to lay out the 2½in (6.4cm) squares of fabric. The various colours alternate with GP20SL. Sew the squares into rows and then sew the rows together.

Sew a large PJ80MV triangle to each side of the chequerboard.

Border 1

Arrange the GP149LV blossoms as in the photo (or choose the blossoms you like best) and alternate the blossom triangles with the large GP150SP triangles.

Following the Border 1 Diagram, sew 3 GP149LV triangles to 4 of the GP150SP triangles, and end with smaller GP149LV triangles.

For the corners, select 2 GP150SP triangles and sew them together to make a mitre, as shown. Repeat to sew 4 sets in total.

Sew two of the pieced borders to the sides of the quilt. Sew GP150SP mitred squares to each end of the remaining two borders, orienting the direction as in the photo and sew these longer borders to the top and bottom of the quilt.

Border 2
Sew the shorter lengths of GP143VN to the sides of the quilt. Sew the longer lengths to the top and bottom of the quilt.

Border 3
Using GP71WS and PJ80MV for each of the 4 borders, alternate 11 pairs of the larger triangles of GP71WS with 12 PJ80MV squares as in the Border 3 Diagram. On each end of the border, sew on 2 of the smaller 3⅞in (9.8cm) half-square triangles. Make 4 corner blocks using a PJ80MV square with small 3⅞in (9.8cm) half-square triangles sewn to each side, as shown.
Sew two pieced borders to each side of the quilt. Sew a corner square to each end of the other two pieced borders and then sew these borders to the top and bottom of the quilt.

Border 4
Using GP54SC sew the shorter lengths to the sides of the quilt. Sew the remaining lengths to the top and bottom of the quilt.

FINISHING THE QUILT
Press the quilt top and the piece of backing fabric. Layer the quilt top, batting and backing, and baste together (see page 156).
Using machine quilting thread, quilt as desired.
Trim the quilt edges and attach the binding to the quilt (see page 157).

QUILT ASSEMBLY DIAGRAM

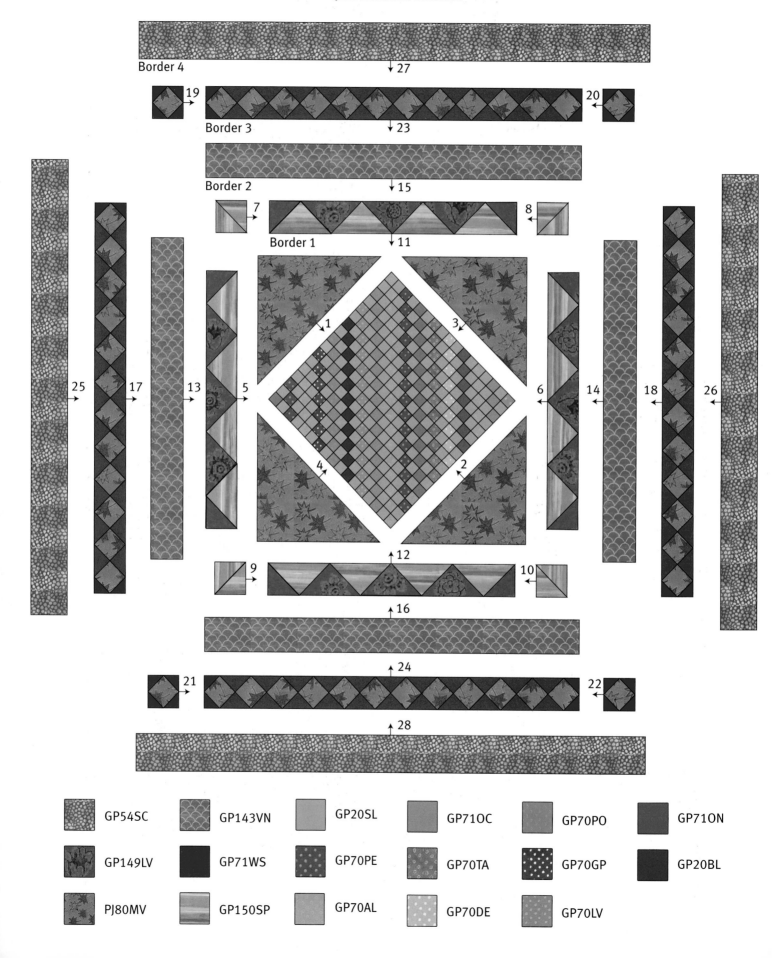

Border 4

Border 3

Border 2

Border 1

GP54SC

GP143VN

GP20SL

GP71OC

GP70PO

GP71ON

GP149LV

GP71WS

GP70PE

GP70TA

GP70GP

GP20BL

PJ80MV

GP150SP

GP70AL

GP70DE

GP70LV

pine bark ***

Janet Haigh

To make this quilt successfully you need to be an experienced quilter who likes a challenge! There are two main blocks, Block 1 and Block 2, and these are also made in a reversed form. The two versions of each block are rotated 180 degrees in specific areas of the quilt layout to achieve the pine bark pattern. Striped fabrics are used to enhance the pine bark shapes but using a non-directional fabric would be easier if you prefer. The quilt uses foundation paper piecing to make Block 1, and although this technique has some fabric wastage, it does create accurate and reliable results. The simpler Block 2, which only occurs in the two rows in the centre of the quilt, is pieced using individual templates. The quilt has been hand quilted and also tied using a variegated perle thread. The instructions for the quilt are slightly different to the quilt shown, but will make the quilt easier to piece.

SIZE OF QUILT

The finished quilt will measure approx.
65in x 80in (165cm x 203cm)

MATERIALS

Fabrics calculated at minimum width of fabric of approx. 40in (101.6cm), unless otherwise stated

Patchwork Fabrics

SHOT COTTON
Sprout	SC94	2⅝yd (2.4m)
Prune	SC03	2⅝yd (2.4m)

WOVEN ALTERNATING STRIPE
Orange	WASOR	1¼yd (1.2m)
Lavender	WASLV	1¼yd (1.2m)

WOVEN BROAD STRIPE
Sunset	WBSSS	2⅛yd (2m)

WOVEN CATERPILLAR STRIPE
Dusk	WCSDU	½yd (45cm)

WOVEN EXOTIC STRIPE
Earth	WESER	2⅛yd (2m)

WOVEN MULTI STRIPE
Lime	WMSLM	1¼yd (1.2m)
Raspberry	WMSRS	1¼yd (1.2m)

Backing Fabric

MIGRATION
Black	BM58BK	5yd (4.6m) of

standard width fabric

Binding

WOVEN CATERPILLAR STRIPE
Dusk	WCSDU	⅝yd (60cm)

Batting

69 x 84in (175cm x 213cm) if hand quilted;
73in x 88in (185cm x 223cm) if machine quilted

Quilting Thread

If hand quilting: hand quilting thread, plus 8 skeins Cotton Perle No.5 variegated for ties
If machine quilting: machine quilting thread

BLOCK 1 TOP AND BOTTOM FOUNDATION PAPERS

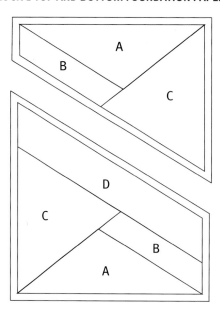

BLOCK 1 TOP AND BOTTOM REVERSE FOUNDATION PAPERS

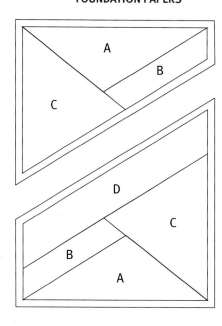

TEMPLATES FOR BLOCK 2

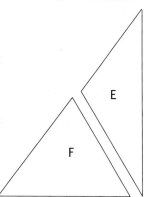

TEMPLATES FOR BLOCK 2 REVERSE

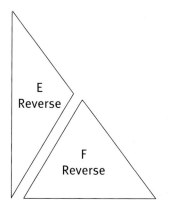

Tip

Before using the fabrics, use spray starch to stabilise them. When cutting out the various pieces, keep the shapes in piles and label them with the letter and the fabric colour or code, so it's easier to find the correct piece later.

CUTTING OUT

BORDER

From SC03 and SC94 cut a piece 5½in x 65½in (14cm x 166.4cm) from the *length* of the fabric.

BLOCK 1 AND BLOCK 1 REVERSE

The pieces cut for foundation paper piecing Block 1 and Block 1 Reverse are cut larger than the shapes seen on the foundation papers to allow for seams and make it easier to piece.

Shape A Cut pieces 3½in x 8in (9cm x 20.3cm). Fabric stripes are used *horizontally*. (Note: the woven striped fabrics are reversible.)
Cut 10 in SC03 and 10 in SC94.
Cut 20 in WASOR, 20 in WASLV, 20 in WMSLM, 20 in WMSRS, 30 in WBSSS and 30 in WESER.
Total of 160 of shape A needed.

Shape B Cut pieces 2½in x 5½in (6.4cm x 14cm).
Cut 80 in SC03 and 80 in SC94.
Total of 160 of shape B needed.

Shape C Cut pieces 7in x 7in (17.8cm x 17.8cm). Fabric stripes are used *vertically*.
Cut 10 in SC03 and 10 in SC94.
Cut 20 in WASOR, 20 in WASLV, 20 in WMSLM, 20 in WMSRS, 30 in WBSSS and 30 in WESER.
Total of 160 of shape C needed.

Shape D Cut pieces 2½in x 11in (6.4cm x 28cm).
Cut 40 in SC03 and 40 in SC94.
Total of 80 of shape D needed.

BLOCK 2 AND BLOCK 2 REVERSE

The pieces for Block 2 and Block 2 Reverse are cut using the templates given (seam allowances included). These blocks only occur in the centre two rows of the quilt.

Shape E Use Template E to cut the following patches. Fabric stripes are used *horizontally*. Cut strips 2⅞in (7.3cm) x width of fabric. You will get 9 shapes from each strip if the template is rotated 180 degrees alternately.
Cut 20 in WCSDU, 10 in WESER and 10 in WBSSS.
Total of 40 of template E needed.

Shape F Use Template F to cut the following patches. Fabric stripes are used *vertically*. Cut strips 4⅜in (11.1cm) x width of fabric. You will get 12 shapes from each strip if the template is rotated 180 degrees alternately.
Cut 20 in WCSDU, 10 in WESER and 10 in WBSSS.
Total of 40 of template F needed.

FABRIC COMBINATIONS

The fabric combinations for the 10 horizontal rows are as follows (see also quilt assembly diagram).
Row 1: SC03, SC94, WESER.
Row 2: SC94, WESER, WASLV.
Row 3: SC94, WASLV, WMSRS.
Row 4: SC94, WMSRS, WBSSS.
Row 5: WBSSS, WCSDU.
Row 6: WCSDU, WESER.
Row 7: SCO3, WESER, WASOR.
Row 8: SC03, WASOR, WMSLM.
Row 9: SC03, WMSLM, WBSSS.
Row 10: SC03, SC94, WMSSS.

MAKING BLOCK 1

Make 40 copies of Block 1 Top Foundation Paper and 40 of Block 1 Bottom Foundation Paper. Photocopy each paper accurately and cut out about ¼in (6mm) past the outer line. Note: the papers are supplied in reverse, so when the block is sewn on the back of the paper it will end up the correct way round.

Collect together the fabric pieces needed for one block, checking against the fabric combinations list.

Starting with the Block 1 Bottom Paper, turn the copy of the foundation paper to the wrong side (see Block 1 Piecing Diagram 1 overleaf) and place the A fabric piece right side up over the piece A shape. Make sure the stripes are running in the correct direction and that the fabric extends past the paper shape on all sides by more than ¼in (6mm). Hold the work up to the light to make sure the fabric is covering the shape. Place the B fabric piece right side down on top, with its long edge extending at least ¼in (6mm) past the proposed seam line. Pin the pieces together temporarily along the proposed seam line to check that when the B piece is sewn and flipped it will cover the B shape.

Turn the work to the right side and re-position the pins, ready for sewing. Reduce your stitch length to about 1.5 and sew the seam line between pieces A and B, extending the stitches past the line at both ends (Diagram 2).

Fold the paper out of the way and with the paper side up, trim the fabric seam allowance to ¼in (6mm) and press the seam (Diagram 3).

Turn the work back to the wrong side and place the C fabric piece right side down over pieces A and B (Diagram 4). Make sure the fabric extends past the paper shape on all sides by more than ¼in (6mm). Pin the work temporarily along the proposed seam line. Check, too, that the stripes (if any) will be running in the correct direction once the piece is sewn. You may need to re-position the fabric a few times to get the stripes running correctly.

Turn the work to the right side and re-position the pins, ready for sewing. Sew the seam line between pieces A and C, extending the stitches past the line at both ends (Diagram 5). Trim the seam allowance to ¼in (6mm), as before, and then press the seam (Diagram 6).

Repeat the foundation piecing process to add the D fabric piece (Diagram 7). Press this bottom half of the block.

Turn the work over and use a rotary cutter and ruler to trim the unit on the outer line (Diagram 8). Carefully remove the paper from the fabric.

Make the top half of Block 1 using the correct fabric pieces and the Block 1 Top Foundation Paper. Use the same process as before to sew and trim the unit but this time using just pieces A, B and C. Remove the paper once sewn.

BLOCK 1 PIECING DIAGRAM

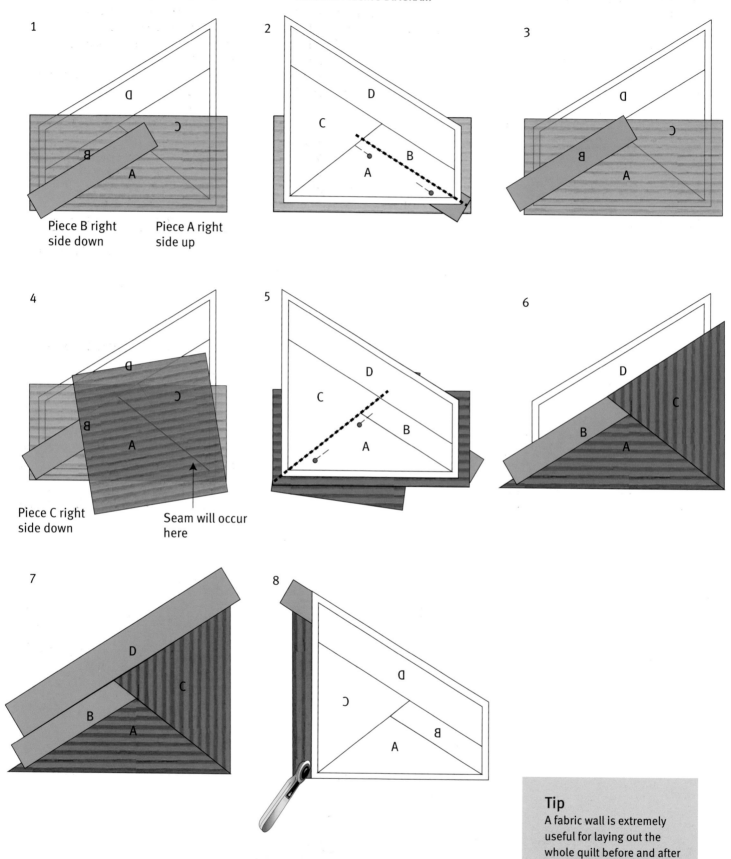

1

Piece B right
side down

Piece A right
side up

2

3

4

Piece C right
side down

Seam will occur
here

5

6

7

8

Tip
A fabric wall is extremely
useful for laying out the
whole quilt before and after
stitching the various blocks.

Take the two halves of the block and sew them together, offsetting the seams by ¼in (6mm) at each end. This will make a block that is 7in (17.8cm) wide x 8in (20.3cm) high. See Block 1 Assembly Diagram.

Make 40 blocks like this in total. For the correct fabric placement follow the fabric combinations list and the Quilt Assembly Diagram.

MAKING BLOCK 1 REVERSE

Make 40 copies of Block 1 Top Reverse Foundation Paper and 40 of Block 1 Bottom Reverse Foundation Paper.
Make these blocks in exactly the same way as Block 1 but using the reverse foundation papers.
Sew the two halves of the block together as before. Make 40 blocks in total.

MAKING BLOCK 2 AND BLOCK 2 REVERSE

There are 10 of Block 2 and 10 of Block 2 Reverse in the quilt. Each block is 7in x 5½in (17.8cm x 14cm) unfinished.
Row 5 has 10 blocks – 5 of Block 2, alternating with 5 of Block 2 Reverse. The blocks in this row use stripe fabrics WCSDU and WBSSS.
Row 6 has 10 blocks – 5 of Block 2 Reverse (rotated 180 degrees at quilt assembly), alternating with 5 of Block 2 (rotated 180 degrees at quilt assembly). The blocks in this row use stripe fabrics WCSDU and WESER.
To make Block 2 use Block 2 Templates E and F – two of each for one block.
To make Block 2 Reverse use Block 2 Templates Reverse E and Reverse F – two of each for one block.

To make a Block 2 use 2 striped patches in WCSDU and 2 striped patches in WBSSS cut from Templates E and F. Make sure the stripes are running in the correct direction.
Following the Block 2 Assembly Diagram, take a triangle E and a triangle F. With right sides together and offsetting the pieces by ⅛in (3mm), sew them together. This makes a large right-angled triangle. Repeat using the other E and F triangles.
Now sew the large triangles together along the diagonal seam, offsetting the pieces by ⅛in (3mm). The centre seam will run from top left to bottom right for this block. Check the block is 7in x 5½in (17.8cm x 14cm).
Make 10 of Block 2 in total.

BLOCK 1 ASSEMBLY DIAGRAM

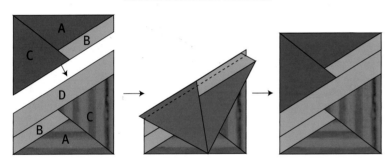

BLOCK 1 REVERSE ASSEMBLY DIAGRAM

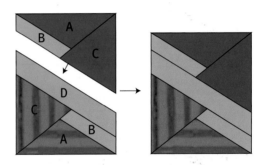

BLOCK 2 ASSEMBLY DIAGRAM

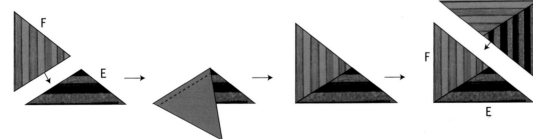
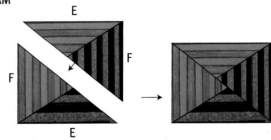

BLOCK 2 REVERSE ASSEMBLY DIAGRAM

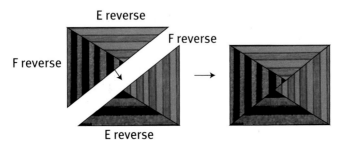

BLOCK 1 PATTERN DIAGRAM

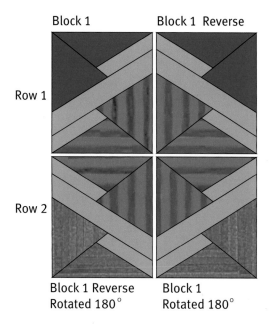

Block 1   Block 1 Reverse

Row 1

Row 2

Block 1 Reverse
Rotated 180°

Block 1
Rotated 180°

BLOCK 2 PATTERN DIAGRAM

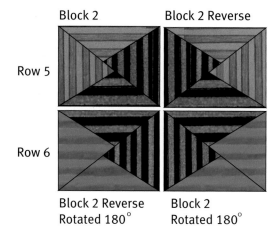

Block 2   Block 2 Reverse

Row 5

Row 6

Block 2 Reverse
Rotated 180°

Block 2
Rotated 180°

To make Block 2 Reverse, follow the instructions for Block 2 but use patches of WCSDU and WESER, cut from Template E Reverse and F Reverse. The centre seam will run from top right to bottom left for this reversed block.

Make 10 of Block 2 Reverse in total.

ASSEMBLING THE QUILT
The quilt is assembled in 10 rows, each with 10 blocks – see the Quilt Assembly Diagram. The rows work in pairs, with four blocks creating a diamond pattern – see Block 1 Pattern Diagram and Block 2 Pattern Diagram. Note that blocks in alternate rows are rotated 180 degrees to achieve the pattern.

Following this pattern carefully and the Quilt Assembly Diagram, lay out all of blocks in 10 rows. Sew each row together. Now sew the rows together. To add the borders, sew a 5½in x 65½in (14cm x 166.4cm) border of SC03 to the top of the quilt and a 5½in x 65½in (14cm x 166.4cm) border of SC94 to the bottom of the quilt.

FINISHING THE QUILT
Using a ¼in (6mm) seam allowance, sew the backing pieces together along the long side and trim to a piece approximately 73in x 88in (185.5cm x 223.5cm).

Layer the quilt top, batting and backing, and baste together (see page 156). Quilt as desired. The quilt shown was hand quilted and hand tied as follows. Hand quilt with toning hand quilting thread in the ditch of all vertical and horizontal seams. Hand quilt with No.5 toning variegated perle thread in the ditch of each pine bark shape.

Work tied quilting (see page 156) using eight strands doubled of No.5 variegated perle thread at the joining points of all the pine bark shapes (see quilt photo on page 105). Tie with a double knot. Trim the quilt edges and attach the binding (see page 157).

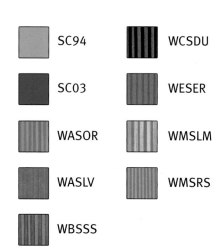

SC94   WCSDU

SC03   WESER

WASOR   WMSLM

WASLV   WMSRS

WBSSS

QUILT ASSEMBLY DIAGRAM

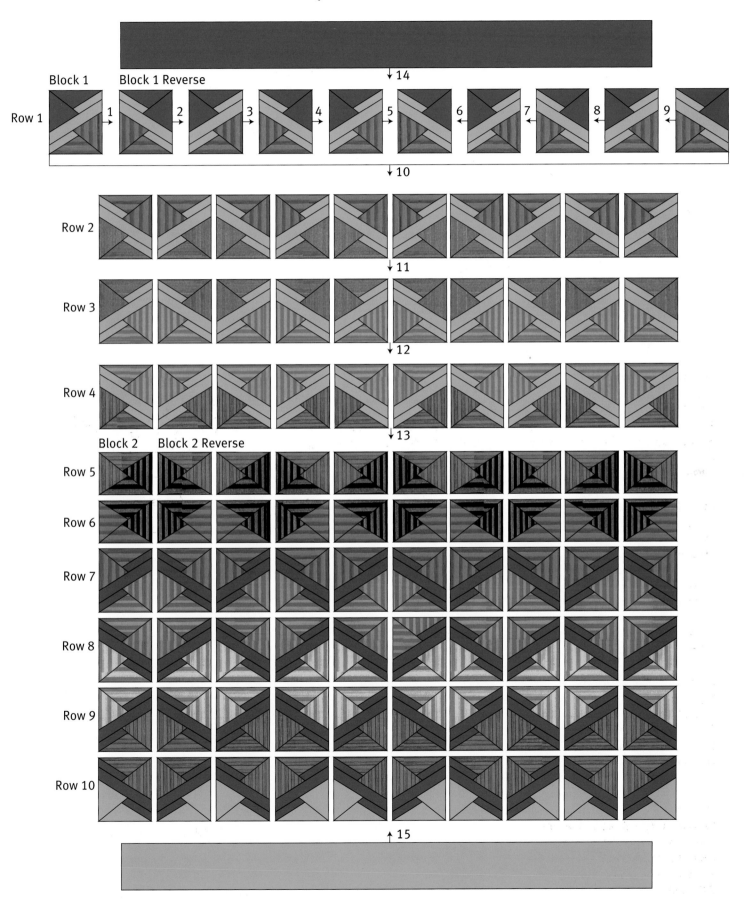

hourglass **

Corienne Kramer

This scrappy quilt is made up of 8in (20.3cm) blocks (finished), with random placement of the fabrics. It is not necessary to place each fabric in the same position as in the original, just be sure to keep the light, medium and dark colours in the right places. This pattern was used in quilts dating from the late 1900s. By clever placing of the dark and light fabrics the blocks take on an hourglass look.

SIZE OF QUILT
The finished quilt will measure approx. 91in x 91in (231cm x 231cm)

MATERIALS
Fabrics calculated at minimum width of fabric of approx. 40in (101.6cm) unless otherwise stated

Patchwork Fabrics
Dark fabrics
JAPANESE CHRYSANTHEMUM
Antique	PJ041AN	½yd (45cm)

MAD PLAID
Charcoal	BM37CC	⅜yd (35cm)

ROMAN GLASS
Purple	GP01PU	⅜yd (35cm)

STRATA
Black	GP150BK	½yd (45cm)

ZANY
Dark	PJ79DK	½yd (45cm)

SPOT
Plum	GP70PL	¼yd (25cm)

PODS
Wine	BM54WN	⅜yd (35cm)

Medium fabrics
FERNS
Periwinkle	GP147PE	⅜yd (35cm)

PAPERWEIGHT
Blue	GP20BL	⅜yd (35cm)

ELEPHANT FLOWERS
Blue	BM56BL	⅜yd (35cm)

MILLEFIORE
Aqua	GP92AQ	⅜yd (35cm)

GUINEA FLOWER
Cobalt	GP59CB	½yd (45cm)

TREE FUNGI
Lavender	PJ82LV	2⅝yd (2.4m)

Light fabrics
MILLEFIORE
Grey   GP92GY   2¼yd (2.1m)
FERNS
Grey   GP147GY   ¾yd (70cm)
SPOT
Silver   GP70SV   ¾yd (70cm)

Backing Fabric
ROMAN GLASS
Lavender   GP01LV   7¼yd (6.6m) of
standard width fabric
OR
MILLEFIORE
Pink   GP92PK   7¼yd (6.6m) of
standard width fabric

Border and Binding Fabric
TREE FUNGI
Lavender   PJ82LV   2⅝yd (2.4m)

Batting
99in x 99in (251cm x 251cm)

Quilting thread
Machine quilting thread

CUTTING OUT
Border and binding
First cut the border and binding from Tree
Fungi Lavender PJ82LV along the length of
yardage, as follows.
Cut 2 strips 6in x 80½in (15.2cm x
204.5cm) for the side borders and 2 strips
6in x 91½in (15.2cm x 232.4cm) for the
top and bottom borders, and set aside.
Cut 4 strips 2½in (6.4cm) wide for
binding, and set aside.

Blocks
Dark fabrics From each of the dark fabrics
cut one 2½in (6.4cm) strip across the
fabric width. Cut each strip into 2½in
(6.4cm) squares (yielding 16 squares per
strip). You need 100 assorted dark 2½in
(6.4cm) squares.
Cut the remainder of the dark fabrics
(except GP70PL, which is only used for

2½in squares) into 4⅞in (12.4cm) strips.
Cut these strips into 4⅞in (12.4cm)
squares (yielding 8 squares per strip).
Cut each square across the diagonal once
into 2 half-square triangles. You need
200 assorted dark half-square triangles
in total.

Medium fabrics From the medium fabrics
cut 2½in (6.4cm) strips across the fabric
width. Cut the strips into 2½in (6.4cm)
squares. You need 300 assorted medium
2½in (6.4cm) squares in total.

Light fabrics From GP92GY cut 7 strips
2½in (6.4cm) across the fabric width.
Cut each strip into 2½in (6.4cm) squares
(yielding 16 squares per strip).
From the remaining light fabrics cut 2½in
(6.4cm) strips across the fabric width.
Cut the strips into 2½in (6.4cm) squares
to yield 300 assorted light 2½in (6.4cm)
squares. Put these squares with 100
PJ92GY light squares cut earlier so you
have 400 assorted light 2½in (6.4cm)
squares in total.
From the Millefiore Grey (GP92GY) cut 13
strips 4⅞in (12.4cm) across the fabric
width. Cut each strip into 4⅞in (12.4cm)
squares (yielding 8 squares per strip).
Cut these in half on the diagonal once
to make half-square triangles. You need
200 GP92GY half-square triangles.

Backing
Cut two pieces 99in x 40in (251.5cm x
101.6cm) and three pieces 20in x 40in
(50.8cm x 101.6cm).

MAKING THE BLOCKS
Use a ¼in (6mm) seam allowance
throughout.
There are 100 blocks in the quilt and
each block has the following units:
4 light colour squares 2½in x 2½in
(6.4cm x 6.4cm).
3 medium colour squares 2½in x 2½in
(6.4cm x 6.4cm).

1 dark colour square 2½in x 2½in (6.4cm
x 6.4cm).
2 dark colour half-square triangles.
2 light colour half-square triangles.

To make a block, follow the Block
Assembly Diagram. Make 2 four-patch
blocks using the dark, light and medium
squares shown in the diagram. Make 2
dark/light half-square triangle units by
sewing the triangles together. Sew the
units together to complete the block.
Make 100 blocks in total.

MAKING THE QUILT
The blocks need to be carefully placed
to achieve the hourglass appearance.
Follow the Quilt Assembly Diagram
carefully, laying out 10 rows each with
10 blocks. Note that alternate blocks are
rotated 90 degrees. Placing the blocks
on a design wall is helpful so that they
can be rotated into the correct positions
before sewing.
Sew the blocks together in rows, as in the
Quilt Assembly Diagram. Now sew the
rows together.
Add the border to the quilt by sewing the
shorter strips of PJ82LV to the sides of
the quilt and then the longer strips to the
top and bottom.

FINISHING THE QUILT
Press the quilt top. Using a ¼in (6mm)
seam allowance, sew the three 20in
x 40in (50.8cm x 101.6cm) pieces of
backing fabric together to make one long
strip. Trim to 99in (251.5cm). Sew this
between the two 99in x 40in (251.5cm
x 101.6cm) pieces of backing fabric to
make a piece 99in x 99in (251.5cm x
251.5cm) approx.
Layer the quilt top, batting and backing,
and baste together (see page 156).
Trim the quilt edges and attach the
binding (see page 157).

BLOCK ASSEMBLY DIAGRAM

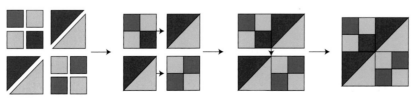

QUILT ASSEMBLY DIAGRAM

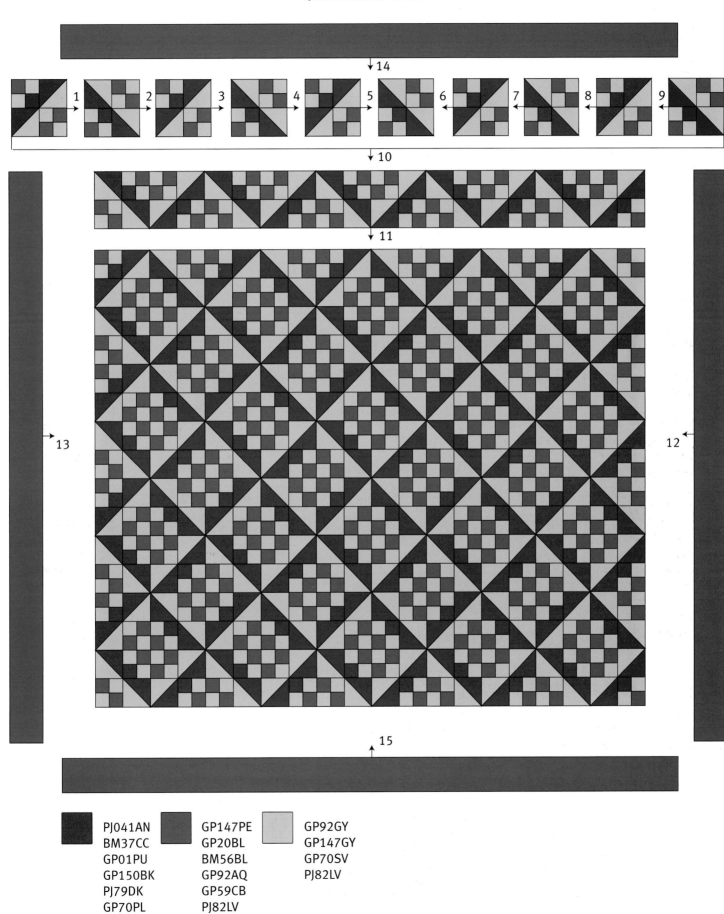

	PJ041AN		GP147PE		GP92GY
	BM37CC		GP20BL		GP147GY
	GP01PU		BM56BL		GP70SV
	GP150BK		GP92AQ		PJ82LV
	PJ79DK		GP59CB		
	GP70PL		PJ82LV		
	BM54WN				

hugs and kisses *

Liza Prior Lucy

This quilt is very simple. The raw-edged, fused noughts and crosses in alternating warm- and cool-coloured fabrics are appliquéd with machine blanket stitch, making it a quick project and perfect for a child's room. If you wish, you could make a baby quilt using fewer blocks.

SIZE OF QUILT
The finished quilt will measure approx. 51in x 68in (129.5cm x 172.7cm)

MATERIALS
Fabrics calculated at minimum width of fabric of approx. 40in (101.6cm), unless otherwise stated

Patchwork fabrics
PUZZLE
Ecru   BM57EC   3¼yd (3m)

¼yd (25cm) of each of the following:
Cool colours
SPOT
Periwinkle   GP70PE
Grape   GP70GP
Turquoise   GP70TQ
ROMAN GLASS
Blue/white   GP01BL
JUMBLE
Turquoise   BM53TQ
Moss   BM53MS

¼yd (25cm) of each of the following:
Warm colours
SPOT
Gold   GP70GD
Fuchsia   GP70FU
ROMAN GLASS
Gold   GP01GD
JUMBLE
Orange   BM53OR
Pink   BM53PK
Tangerine   BM53TN

Backing fabric
PODS
Sky   BM54SK   3½yd (3.2m)
of standard width fabric

Batting
59in x 76in (150cm x 193cm)

Binding
ABORIGINAL DOT
Cantaloupe GP71CA   ½yd (45cm)

Quilting thread
Machine quilting thread

Blanket stitching thread
1 spool 40wt brightly coloured cotton thread

Fusible web
Lightweight fusible web (paper on both sides recommended) approx. 5yd (4.6m) long x 18in (45.7cm) wide

Template Plastic
Approx. 8in x 16in (20.3cm x 40.6cm)

TEMPLATES
Trace one X-shaped template and one O-shaped template onto template plastic and cut out the shapes. Note: no seam allowance is needed.

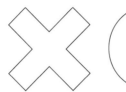

CUTTING OUT
From BM57EC cut 48 squares 9in (22.9cm).
Leave the cool-coloured and warm-coloured fabrics uncut for the moment. Trace around the plastic templates onto one side of the fusible web, and draw 24 'X' templates and 24 'O' templates. Cut out each drawn template approx. ⅛in (3mm) beyond the drawn lines.
Remove the paper from the other side of the fusible web and fuse 4 'X' pieces of fusible web onto the wrong side of each of the cool-coloured fabrics. You can place the shapes close together.
Fuse 4 'O' pieces of fusible web on the wrong side of each of the warm-coloured fabrics.
Cut out the shapes on the drawn line. Do not remove the paper backing until ready to sew.

Backing
Cut the BM54SK fabric in half to make two pieces each approx. 60in (152.4cm) long.

Binding
Cut seven strips 2½in (6.4cm) wide across the width of the fabric in GP71CA.

MAKING THE QUILT
Use a ¼in (6mm) seam allowance throughout.
Crease each BM57EC square in half diagonally both ways to find the centre for the 'X' and 'O' appliqué patches. Remove the backing paper from each 'X' and 'O' as you go, and, following the directions that come with the fusible web, centre the appliqué onto the right side of the square and press with a hot iron until fused.
Using a machine blanket stitch, stitch around all the edges of all the 'X' and 'O' patches. If your machine doesn't have blanket stitch you could use a zig zag or satin stitch instead.
Referring to the quilt photo and Quilt Assembly Diagram for colour placement, alternate the 'O' blocks with the 'X' blocks and sew the blocks into rows. Now sew the rows together.

FINISHING THE QUILT
Press the quilt top. Remove the selvedges from the backing fabric pieces and sew together to make one piece approx. 60in x 76in (152.4cm x 193cm).
Layer the quilt top, batting and backing, and baste together (see page 156).
Using machine quilting thread, quilt as desired.
Trim the quilt edges and attach the binding (see page 157).

Tip
If you like hand embroidery you could use a hand blanket stitch to edge the appliqués, using a thick perle cotton or several strands of a stranded cotton embroidery thread.

QUILT ASSEMBLY DIAGRAM

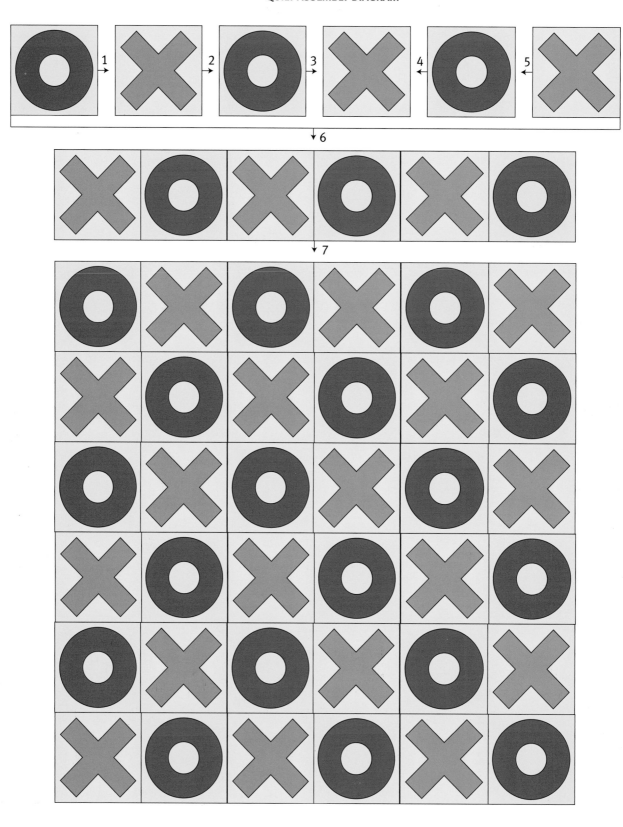

BM57EC

GP70PE
GP70GP
GP70TQ
GP01BL
BM53TQ
BM53MS

GP70GD
GP70FU
GP01GD
BM53OR
BM53PK
BM53TN

garden lattice **

Sally Davis

This quilt is created from an assortment of 15 hot-coloured print fabrics contrasting with a pea green Shot Cotton fabric. The arrangement is created with a single block pattern, with alternate blocks rotated to make a lattice pattern. It is also pieced with intersecting sashing, so it looks more intricate than it actually is. It is best to use the red/pink prints randomly to give an attractive scrappy look to the quilt.

SIZE OF QUILT
The finished quilt measures approx 68in x 84in (173cm x 214cm).

MATERIALS
Fabrics calculated at minimum width of fabric of approx. 40in (101.6cm), unless otherwise stated

Patchwork fabrics
SHOT COTTON
Pea green   SC91   2½yd (2.3m)

Red/pink prints
⅜yd (35cm) of each of the following
STRIPED HERALDIC
Red   GP153RD
ZANY
Hot   PJ79HT
BROCADE PEONY
Autumn   PJ62AU
Red   PJ62RD
Wine   PJ62WN
MIGRATION
Pink   BM58PK
TREE FUNGI
Pink   PJ82PK
SHAGGY
Red   PJ72RD
PAPERWEIGHT
Red   GP20RD
Paprika   GP20PP
BRASSICA
Rust   PJ51RU
LOTUS LEAF
Wine   GP29WN
LAKE BLOSSOM
Red   GP93RD
LEOPARD LOTUS
Ochre   PJ81OC
GUINEA FLOWER
Red   GP59RD   ⅞yd (60cm)

Backing fabric
CARPET
Green   QBGP01GN   2³⁄₈yd (2.2m)
of 108in (274cm) wide fabric

Binding
GUINEA FLOWER
Red   GP59RD   ³⁄₄yd (70cm)

Batting
76in x 92in (193cm x 234cm)

Quilting thread
Machine quilting thread

PATCHES
A single block design is used throughout
the quilt, made up of assorted 2½in
(6.4cm) squares in red/pink prints, 2½in
(6.4cm) squares in pea green (SC91) and
right-angled triangles in red/pink prints
and pea green (SC91), cut from 2⅞in
(7.3cm) squares.

CUTTING OUT
Blocks
From SC91 cut 20 strips 2½in (6.4cm) x
width of fabric. Cut each strip into 2½in
(6.4cm) squares (16 per strip width), for a
total of 320 squares.

From SC91 cut 12 strips 2⅞in (7.3cm) x
width of fabric. Cut each strip into 2⅞in
(7.3cm) squares (14 per strip width), for
a total of 160 squares. Cut each square in
half along the diagonal once for a total of
320 triangles.

From the 15 assorted red/pink prints cut
2½in (6.4cm) x width of fabric strips (for
a total of 40 strips). From these strips cut
2½in (6.4cm) squares (you can cut 16
from each strip). You will need a total of
640 assorted squares.

From the 15 assorted red/pink prints cut
2⅞in (7.3cm) x width of fabric strips (for
a total of 12 strips). From these strips cut
2⅞in (7.3cm) squares (you can cut 14
from each strip). Cut each square in half
along the diagonal once for a total of 320
assorted triangles.

Sashing
Using GP59RD, cut 8 strips 2½in (6.4cm)
x width of fabric and sew together into
one long strip. From this strip cut the
following:
Cut 2 strips 2½in x 64½in (6.4cm x
163.8cm).
Cut 2 strips 2½in x 68½in (6.4cm x
174cm).
Cut 4 strips 2½in x 8½in (6.4cm x
21.6cm).

Backing
Trim off selvedges and cut a piece 100in
(254cm) wide x 84in (213cm) long in
QBGP01GN.

Binding
Cut 9 strips 2½in (6.4cm) wide in
GP59RD.

MAKING THE BLOCKS
There are 80 blocks in the quilt, all made
the same way. For one block assemble
the following units:
Eight assorted 2½in (6.4cm) squares in
red/pink prints.
Four 2½in (6.4cm) squares in SC91.
Four 2⅞in (7.3cm) triangles in assorted
red/pink prints.
Four 2⅞in (7.3cm) triangles in SC91.
Arrange the units in the pattern shown in
the Block Assembly Diagram. Using ¼in
(6mm) seams, sew the units together
into rows as shown, and then sew the
rows together. The block should be 8½in
(21.6cm) at this stage.
Repeat to make a total of 80 blocks.

MAKING THE QUILT
The lattice pattern is created by the
rotation of alternate blocks. Make the
quilt centre first. Take 48 blocks and
lay them out in 8 rows each with 6
blocks. Rotate alternate blocks to create
the pattern shown in the Quilt Centre
Assembly Diagram. Using ¼in (6mm)
seams, sew each row together, making
sure the pattern remains correct. Now
sew the rows together.
Sew a GP59RD 2½in x 64½in (6.4cm x
163.8cm) sashing strip to both sides of
the quilt.

Add the borders as follows, referring to
the Borders Assembly Diagram (overleaf).
Take 8 blocks and carefully following the
pattern shown in the diagram to rotate
the blocks correctly, sew them together
into a column. Sew this to the left-hand
side of the quilt.
Take another 8 blocks and repeat to
make a column for the right-hand side,
following the pattern carefully. Sew in
place.
Take 8 blocks and 2 GP59RD 2½in x
8½in (6.4cm x 21.6cm) sashing strips
and carefully following the pattern in the
diagram, sew them together into a row.
Repeat with the remaining 8 blocks and 2
GP59RD 2½in x 8½in (6.4cm x 21.6cm)
sashing strips.
Sew a GP59RD 2½in x 68½in (6.4cm x
174cm) sashing strip to the top and the
bottom of the quilt.
Finally, sew the top border and the
bottom border to the quilt.

BLOCK ASSEMBLY DIAGRAM

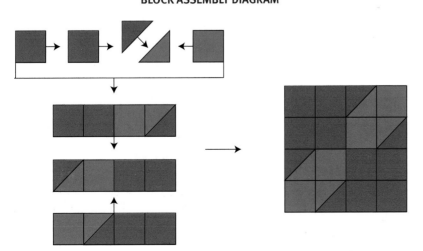

QUILT CENTRE ASSEMBLY DIAGRAM

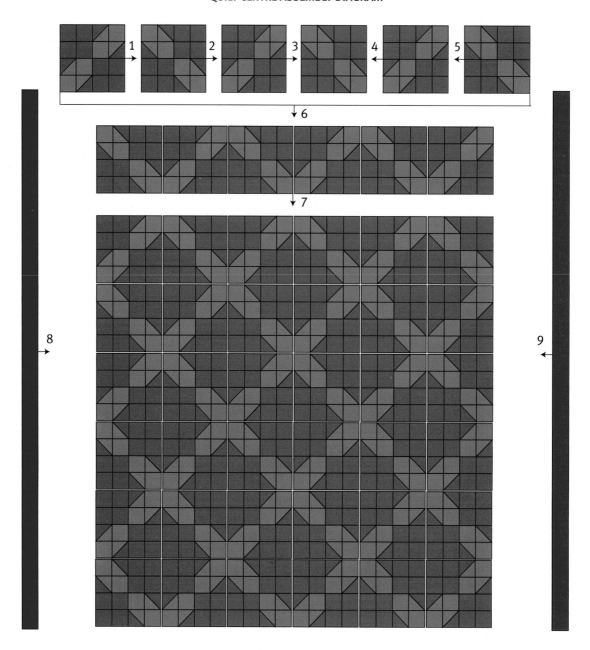

FINISHING THE QUILT

Press the quilt top and the fabric backing piece.

Layer the quilt top, batting and backing, and baste together (see page 156).

Quilt in the ditch as desired using machine quilting thread.

Trim the quilt edges and attach the binding (see page 157).

SC91

GP153RD
PJ79HT
PJ62AU
PJ62RD
PJ62WN
BM58PK
PJ82PK
PJ72RD
GP20RD
GP20PP
PJ51RU
GP29WN
GP93RD
PJ81OC
GP59RD

GP59RD

BORDERS ASSEMBLY DIAGRAM

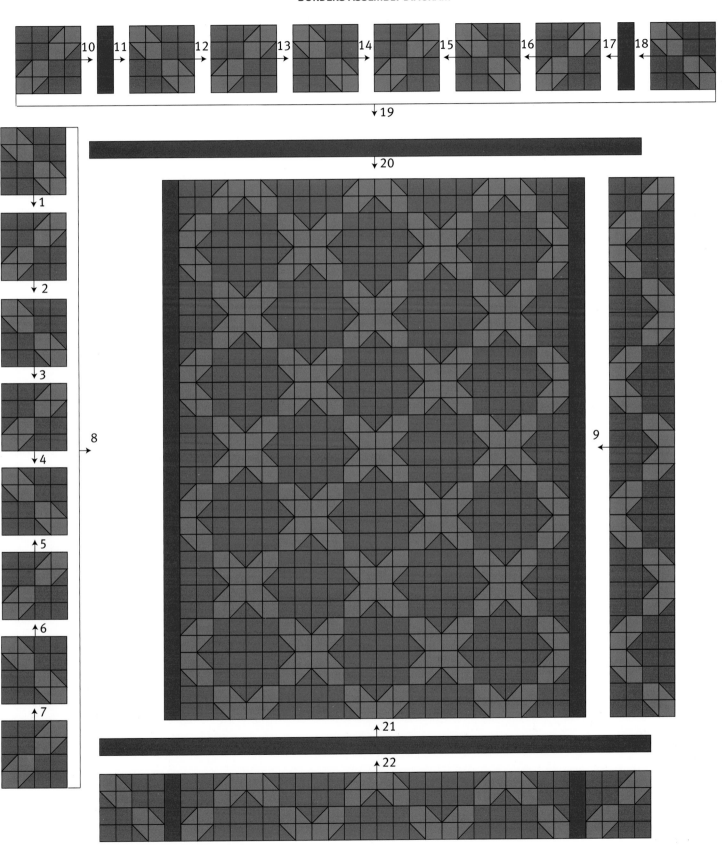

eton mess *

Brandon Mably

This traditional pinwheel block made up of half-square triangle units looks almost edible, hence the name! Whether you decide to follow Brandon's superb colour layout using the photograph or choose your own, this quilt offers endless possibilities by just changing the colours. Treat it as a scrap quilt but keep to a general light/dark arrangement.

SIZE OF QUILT
The finished quilt will measure approx. 75in x 90in (190.5cm x 228.5cm)

MATERIALS
Fabrics calculated at minimum width of fabric of approx. 40in (101.6cm), unless otherwise stated

Patchwork Fabrics
Dark fabrics

GUINEA FLOWER

Apricot	GP59AP	½yd (45cm)
Red	GP59RD	½yd (45cm)

ELEPHANT FLOWER

Orange	BM56OR	½yd (45cm)

MAD PLAID

Red	BM37RD	½yd (45cm)

HEAT WAVE

Tomato	BM55TM	½yd (45cm)
Turquoise	BM55TQ	½yd (45cm)

PUZZLE

Red	BM57RD	½yd (45cm)

STRIPED HERALDIC

Red	GP158RD	¾yd (70cm)

Light fabrics

PUZZLE

White	BM57WH	½yd (45cm)

STRIPED HERALDIC

Pink	GP153PK	¾yd (70cm)

MILLEFIORE

Pink	GP92PK	½yd (45cm)

BUTTON FLOWER

Aqua	GP152AQ	¾yd (70cm)

JUPITER

Pastel	GP131PT	½yd (45cm)

ROMAN GLASS

Pastel	GP01PT	½yd (45cm)

PODS

Sky	BM54SK	¾yd (70cm)

Backing Fabric
PODS

Rose	BM54RO	5⅞yd (5.5m)

of standard width fabric

125

HALF-SQUARE TRIANGLE DIAGRAM

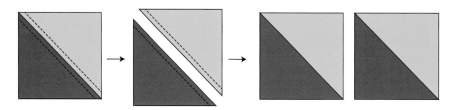

BLOCK ASSEMBLY DIAGRAM

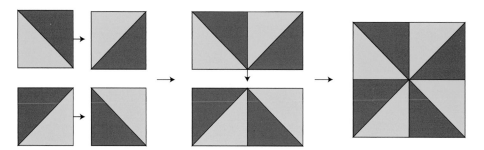

Binding
JUMBLE
Turquoise   BM53TQ   ¾yd (70cm)

Batting
83in x 98in (211cm x 249cm)

Quilting Thread
Machine quilting thread

PATCH SHAPES
The quilt is pieced from simple pinwheel blocks, with each block made by sewing together four half-square triangle units. The placement of the light and dark triangles in each block creates the illusion, once it is sewn together, that the block is spinning. The half-square triangle units are created using a two-at-once method, starting with 9in (22.9cm) squares.

CUTTING OUT
9in (22.9cm) squares
Cut 9in (22.9cm) strips across the fabric width and cut into 9in (22.9cm) squares. Each strip will give 4 squares per fabric width.
Cut 6 squares in BM57RD, BM57WH, BM37RD, GP59AP. Cut 8 in GP92PK, GP131PT, BM56OR, GP59RD, GP01PT, BM55TM, BM55TQ. Cut 10 in BM54SK, GP152AQ, GP158RD and GP153PK. This will give a total of 120 squares.

Binding
Cut 10 strips 2½in (6.4cm) wide across the width of the fabric in BM53TQ.

Backing
In BM54RO cut 2 pieces 40in x 98in (101.6cm x 249cm) and three pieces 4in x 40in (10.2cm x 101.6cm).

MAKING THE BLOCKS
Each pinwheel block is made of 4 half-square triangle (HST) units, made using the same pair of fabrics, a dark and a light. These HSTs are made using a two-at-once method (see Half-square Triangle Diagram).
Place one 9in (22.9cm) square of light fabric and one 9in (22.9cm) square of dark fabric right sides together, matching edges. Mark a diagonal line from corner to corner. Sew ¼in (6mm) away from the marked line on both sides. Cut the units apart on the marked line and press towards the darker fabric. Trim each unit to 8in (20.3cm) square. Repeat this with another light square and dark square to make another two units.
Arrange the four HSTs as shown in the Block Assembly Diagram. Sew the units together in pairs and then sew the pairs together, matching the centre seam, and press.

Repeat this process with all of the dark and light squares to create another 116 HSTs.

MAKING THE QUILT
Use a ¼in (6mm) seam allowance throughout. Assemble the HST units into 30 blocks in total (see Block Assembly Diagram).
Sew the blocks into 6 rows of 5 blocks following the Quilt Assembly Diagram. Sew the rows together to form the quilt centre.

FINISHING THE QUILT
Press the quilt top. Sew the three 4in x 40in (10.2cm x 101.6cm) pieces of backing fabric together end to end using a ¼in (6mm) seam allowance and trim to 98in (249cm) long. Sew a 40in x 98in (101.6cm x 249cm) piece of back fabric to both sides of this narrow strip, to form a backing approx. 83in x 98in (210.8cm x 249cm).
Layer the quilt top, batting and backing, and baste together (see page 156).
Quilt in the ditch of the seams using matching machine quilting thread. Trim the quilt edges and attach the binding (see page 157).

QUILT ASSEMBLY DIAGRAM

■	GP59AP	□	BM57WH
	GP59RD		GP153PK
	BM56OR		GP92PK
	BM37RD		GP152AQ
	BM55TM		GP131PT
	BM55TQ		GP01PT
	BM57RD		BM54SK
	GP158RD		

whirling stripes ***

Liza Prior Lucy

Julie Silber, one of our favourite collectors of antique quilts, had a picture in her kitchen of the fabulous old quilt that inspired this one. Hers was in solids and had many more spokes in the rectangles. I simplified the structure and added striped and Shot cotton fabrics to get this dramatic swirling effect. Paper foundation piecing makes these odd angles easy to do with precision. It does waste quite a bit of fabric but it is worth it to get the stripes to swirl around these blocks.

SIZE OF QUILT
The finished quilt will measure approx. 52½in x 52½in (133cm x 133cm)

MATERIALS
Fabrics calculated at minimum width of fabric of approx. 40in (101.6cm), unless otherwise stated

Patchwork Fabrics
½yd (45cm) each of the following:
SHOT COTTON

Curry	SC84
Lavender	SC14
Sprout	SC94
Chartreuse	SC12
Clementine	SC80
Magenta	SC81
Blueberry	SC88
Eucalyptus	SC90

½yd (45cm) each of the following:
WOVEN CATERPILLAR STRIPE

Yellow	WCSYE
Aqua	WCSAQ
Blue	WCSBL
Dark	WCSDK
Sunshine	WCSSU
Sprout	WCSSR
Tomato	WCSTM
Earth	WCSER

MIGRATION

Dark	BM58DK	1⅝yd (1.5m)

(includes binding)

Backing Fabric
PAPER FANS

Ochre	GP143OC	3½yd (3.2m)

of standard width

Binding
See above

Batting
60in x 60in (152.5cm x 152.5cm)

Quilting Thread
Machine quilting thread

FOUNDATION PAPERS

Foundation Paper A 32 copies
Foundation Paper B 32 copies
To avoid distortion, make all copies directly from the book (not copies from copies)

CUTTING OUT

Blocks

Each block is made up of 4 foundation pieced units (2 A and 2 B) and one 2⅞in (7.3cm) square for the block centre.
Cut 3⅛in (8cm) wide strips from selvedge to selvedge as you need them. Each block can be made with 2 strips from one of the woven stripes and 2 strips from one of the Shot cottons. (You do not need to make the same Shot and Stripe colour combinations as in the original as all the colours go together well.)

Border and Block Centres

From BM58DK, cut the borders first, cutting *length* of fabric strips: cut 2 borders 2½in x 52½in (6.4cm x 133.3cm) and 2 borders 2½in x 48½in (6.4cm x 123.2cm). Then cut 16 squares each 2⅞in x 2⅞in (7.3cm x 7.3cm) for the block centres. Set aside the remaining fabric for binding.

Binding

Using the remaining BM58DK, cut 4 length of fabric 2½in (6.4cm) strips. Sew the strips together end to end. You will need a length of at least 220in (560cm).

Backing

Cut 2 pieces approximately 60in x 40in (152.5cm x 101.6cm).

FOUNDATION PAPER A

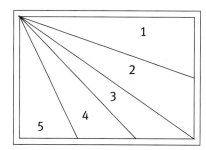

FOUNDATION PAPER B

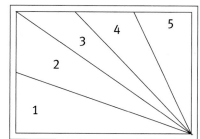

FOUNDATION PIECING DIAGRAM

1

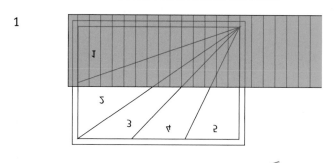

2

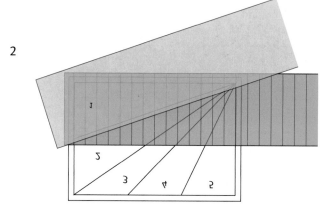

3

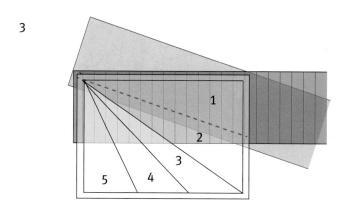

130

MAKING THE BLOCKS

To make one foundation pieced unit, select two 3⅛in (8cm) strips of a Shot cotton fabric and two strips of one Woven Stripe. Set your sewing machine stitch length to a slightly smaller than usual setting to make it easier to tear away the paper later.

On the back of a Foundation Paper A (the side without lines), place the striped fabric (right side up) so that it amply covers the triangle labelled 1. (The stripes should be perpendicular to the long straight bottom edge of the unit.) Be sure to place the fabric beyond the outside edge as it will be trimmed to size when done (see Foundation Piecing Diagram 1). Pin in place (avoiding sewing lines).

Place the Shot cotton strip on top of the Woven stripe as in Diagram 2. Pin in place. Turn the pinned piece over and sew on the line between shapes 1 and 2, starting before the edge and finishing after the edge (diagram 3). Trim the seam allowance to ¼in (6mm). Flip the piece over, fold the Shot cotton open and press. Trim excess Shot cotton and Woven stripe fabric well beyond the outside edges of the paper.

Repeat this basic process, placing the remaining piece of Woven stripe on top of the Shot cotton so that it overlaps beyond the seam line between 2 and 3. Make sure the stripe is perpendicular to that seam line. Pin, sew, trim and press as before. Continue in this manner until all 5 sections are sewn. Press well and then trim to the outer line on the Foundation Paper – this will allow for a ¼in (6mm) seam allowance. The unit will measure 7¾in x 5⅜in (19.7cm x 13.6cm). Do not remove the paper yet.

Using the same process make a second unit using Foundation Paper A.

Using the same process and 2 of Foundation Paper B, make 2 units, but for these start with the Shot cotton covering triangle #1.

To assemble a block, use spray starch to press 2 A units and 2 B units with the paper still attached, and then carefully remove the papers. Handle the pieces gently as the edges are not on the grain. Place the centre square on the first unit and sew a partial seam as in the Partial Seam Diagram. Open and place the second unit on and sew a complete seam. Note: do not worry about which way to press the seams – because of the bulk at the spot where all the points meet, do not try to fold it back. The back behind the centre square will be awkward with the seams allowances twisting.

Following the Block Assembly Diagram, sew the third and fourth units to the centre. Complete the partial seam between the first and fourth patches. Using more spray starch, press very well from the front. This will make the awkward seams around the centre square flatten out.

Repeat this to make 16 blocks in total.

MAKING THE QUILT

Following the Quilt Assembly Diagram, layout out the blocks in 4 rows of 4 blocks, making sure that they are turned so that the Woven stripe fabrics on one block are sewn to the Shot cotton fabrics on the next block.

Sew each row together and press. Now sew the rows together.

Sew the shorter border strips to the sides of the quilt. Sew the longer border strips to the top and bottom.

FINISHING THE QUILT

Press the quilt top. Remove the selvedges from the two backing pieces and seam together along the long edges to make a piece about 60in x 80in (152.4cm x 203cm). Trim to 60in x 60in (152.4cm x 152.4cm).

Layer the quilt top, batting and backing, and baste together (see page 156).

Quilt as desired.

Trim the quilt edges and attach the binding (see page 157).

PARTIAL SEAM DIAGRAM

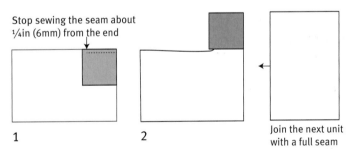

BLOCK ASSEMBLY DIAGRAM

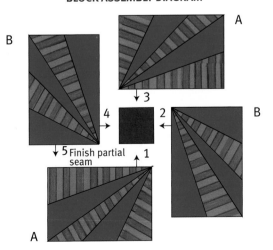

QUILT ASSEMBLY DIAGRAM

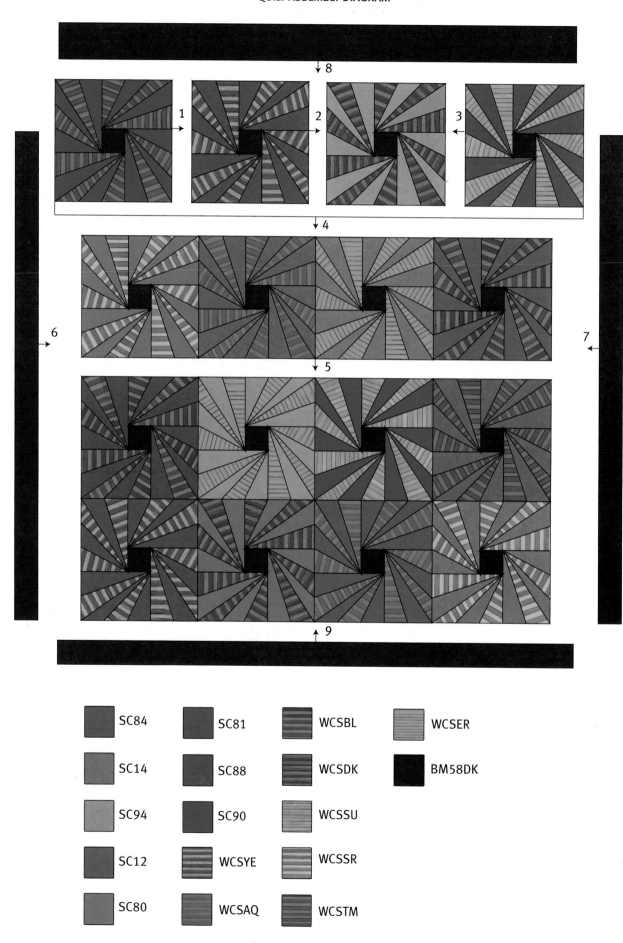

SC84	SC81	WCSBL	WCSER
SC14	SC88	WCSDK	BM58DK
SC94	SC90	WCSSU	
SC12	WCSYE	WCSSR	
SC80	WCSAQ	WCSTM	

square dance **

Julie Stockler

This simple – and simple to make – medallion quilt features a checkerboard centre surrounded by five borders, each made of squares, and finished with a sixth border of 16-patch blocks on point. The design was inspired by a 19th-century American beauty made from blue mattress ticking and red plaids.

SIZE OF QUILT
The finished quilt will measure approx. 80in x 80in (203cm x 203cm)

MATERIALS
Fabrics calculated at minimum width of fabric of approx. 40in (101.6cm), unless otherwise stated

Patchwork Fabrics
ABORIGINAL DOT
Delft	GP71DF	½yd (45cm)
Terra Cotta	GP71TC	⅞yd (80cm)

BUTTON FLOWERS
Aqua	GP152AQ	⅜yd (35cm)

DREAM
Red	GP148RD	½yd (45cm)

FERNS
Periwinkle	GP147PE	1yd (90cm)
Yellow	GP147YE	½yd (45cm)

GUINEA FLOWER
Cobalt	GP59CB	½yd (45cm)

MILLEFIORE
Pastel	GP92PT	⅝yd (60cm)
Tomato	GP92TM	½yd (45cm)

PODS
Gold	BM54GD	⅜yd (35cm)

SPOT
China Blue	GP70CI	1⅝yd (1.5m)
Paprika	GP70PP	⅜yd (35cm)

Backing Fabric
MILLEFIORE
Pastel	GP92PT	5¾yd (5.3m)

of standard width fabric

Binding
PAPERWEIGHT
Blue	GP20BL	⅝yd (60cm)

Batting
88in x 88in (223cm x 223cm)

Quilting Thread
Machine quilting thread

CUTTING OUT

Centre Checkerboard
Cut two 2½in (6.4cm) wide strips in GO20BL and two 2½in (6.4cm) wide strips in GP70PP. From these strips, cut 2½in (6.4cm) squares, to make 32 squares in each fabric.

Border 1
Cut 2 strips 4½in (11.4cm) wide in GP70CI and 2 strips 4½in (11.4cm) wide strips in BM54GD. Cut these strips into 4½in (11.4cm) squares, to make 10 squares in each fabric.

Border 2
Cut 2 strips 8½in (21.6cm) wide in GP147PE and 2 strips 8½in (21.6cm) wide in GP148RD. Cut these strips into 8½in (21.6cm) squares, to make 8 squares in each fabric.

Border 3
Cut 3 strips 4½in (11.4cm) wide in GP70PP and 3 strips 4½in (11.4cm) wide in GP152AQ. Cut these strips into 4½in (11.4cm) squares, to make 22 squares in each fabric.

Border 4
Cut 7 strips 2½in (6.4cm) wide in GP59CB and 7 strips 2½in (6.4cm) wide in GP92TM. Cut these strips into 2½in (6.4cm) squares to make 104 squares in each fabric.

Border 5
Cut 4 strips 4½in (11.4cm) wide in GP92PT and 4 strips 4½in (11.4cm) wide in GP147PE. Cut these strips into 4½in (11.4cm) squares, to make 30 squares in each fabric.

Border 6
Cut 15 strips 2in (5cm) wide in GP71TC. From these strips, cut a total of 288 squares 2in (5cm).
Cut 8 strips 2in (5cm) wide in GP71DF. From these strips, cut 144 squares 2in (5cm).
Cut 8 strips 2in (5cm) wide in GP147YE. From these strips, cut 144 squares 2in (5cm).
Cut 9 strips 4⅞in (12.4cm) wide in GP70CI. Cut these strips into 4⅞in (12.4cm) squares for a total of 72 squares. Cut each square on the diagonal

Tip
Keep the squares you cut for the various borders in separate piles or envelopes so you don't mix them up before assembly.

once to make 2 triangles per square, for a total of 144 triangles.

Backing
Cut two pieces 88in x 40in (223.4cm x 101.6cm) in GP92PT. Cut three pieces 9in x 40in (23cm x 101.6cm).

Binding
Cut 9 strips 2½in (6.4cm) wide in GP20BL.

MAKING THE QUILT
Use a ¼in (6mm) seam allowance throughout and refer to the Quilt Assembly Diagram (overleaf) for fabric placement. For all borders, sew the side borders in place first and press, and then the top and bottom borders and press.

Centre Checkerboard
Stitch the 2½in (6.4cm) squares together in 8 alternating rows of 8 squares each (see Centre Assembly Diagram). Stitch these rows together to form the centre checkerboard. Check the piecing is 16½in (42cm) square.

Border 1
Using the 4½in (11.4cm) squares in an alternating pattern, sew 4 together and sew to the sides of the quilt. Sew 6 together for the top and bottom of the quilt.

Border 2
Using the 8½in (21.6cm) squares in an alternating pattern, sew 3 together and sew to the sides of the quilt. Sew 5 together for the top and bottom of the quilt. Pay attention to the proper orientation of the flowers in the GP148RD fabric.

Border 3
Using the 4½in (11.4cm) squares in an alternating pattern, sew 10 together

134

and sew to the sides of the quilt. Sew 12 together for the top and bottom of the quilt.

Border 4

Sew the squares for Border 4 into 52 4-patch blocks, making each block as shown in the Border 4 Diagram.
Sew 12 blocks together and sew to the sides of the quilt. Sew 14 blocks together and sew to the top and bottom of the quilt.

Border 5

Sew 14 squares together and sew to the sides of the quilt. Sew 16 squares together and sew to the top and bottom of the quilt.

Border 6

All of the on-point 16-patch blocks in this border are made in the same way (see Tip). Lay out 16 2in (5cm) squares as shown in the Border 6 Diagram and sew them together in 4 rows each with 4 squares. Now join the rows together. Trim approximately ⅛in (3mm) from each side of the unit so it measures 6⅜in (16.8cm) square.
Take 4 of the 4⅞in (12.4cm) triangles and sew 2 to opposite sides of the 16-patch block. Press the seams and then sew the other 2 triangles on the remaining sides and press.
Repeat this to make 36 blocks in total.
Sew 8 blocks together for the sides of the quilt and sew in place. Sew 10 blocks together for the top and bottom of the quilt and sew in place. If you rotate the blocks to make each block a different orientation from its neighbour, this will heighten the scrappy effect of the quilt.

Tip

When piecing the 16-patch blocks you could alter the positions of the squares in some blocks if you wish (as done in the quilt shown), and then, when the blocks are sewn together, the blocks can be rotated to heighten the scrappy effect of the quilt.

CENTRE ASSEMBLY DIAGRAM

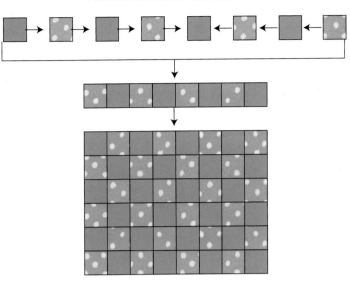

BORDER 4 DIAGRAM

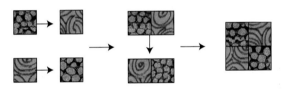

BORDER 6 DIAGRAM

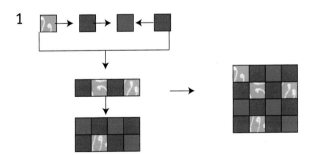

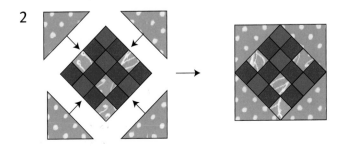

QUILT ASSEMBLY DIAGRAM

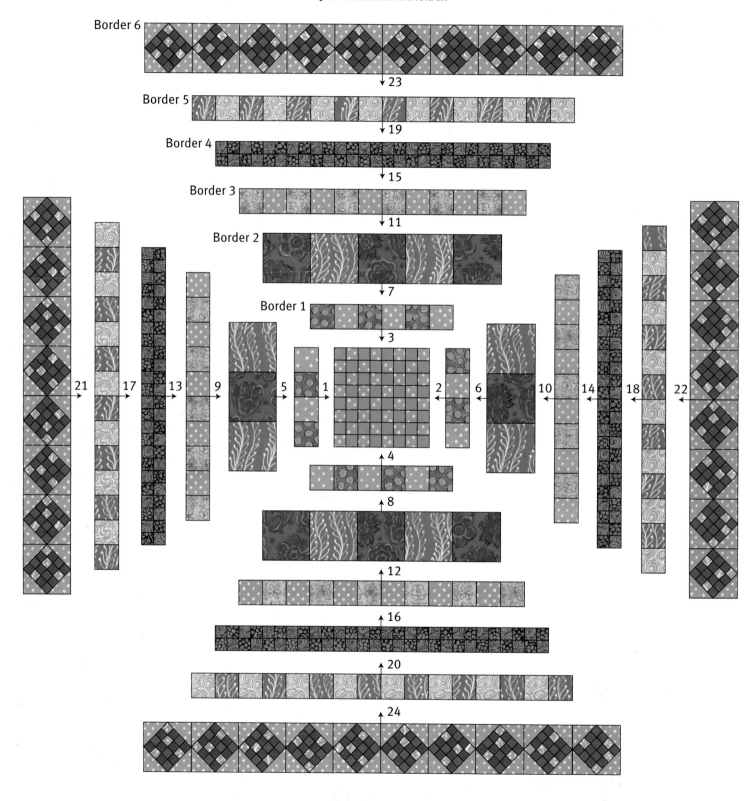

FINISHING THE QUILT

Press the quilt top. Sew the three 9in x 40in (23cm x 101.6cm) pieces of backing fabric together end to end using a ¼in (6mm) seam allowance and trim to 88in (223.4cm) long. Sew a 40in x 88in (101.6cm x 223.4cm) piece of backing fabric to both sides of this narrow strip, to form a backing approx. 88in x 88in (223.4cm x 223.4cm).

Layer the quilt top, batting and backing, and baste together (see page 156). Quilt in the ditch in all seams using matching machine quilting thread. Trim the quilt edges and attach the binding (see page 157).

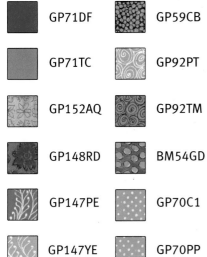

GP71DF	GP59CB
GP71TC	GP92PT
GP152AQ	GP92TM
GP148RD	BM54GD
GP147PE	GP70C1
GP147YE	GP70PP

templates

Refer to the individual quilt instructions for the templates needed. Look for the quilt name on the templates, to make sure you are using the correct shapes for the project. Arrows on templates should be lined up with the straight grain of the fabric, which runs either along the selvedge or at 90 degrees to the selvedge. Following marked grain lines is important to avoid bias edges, which can cause distortion. In some quilts the arrows also denote fabric stripe direction.

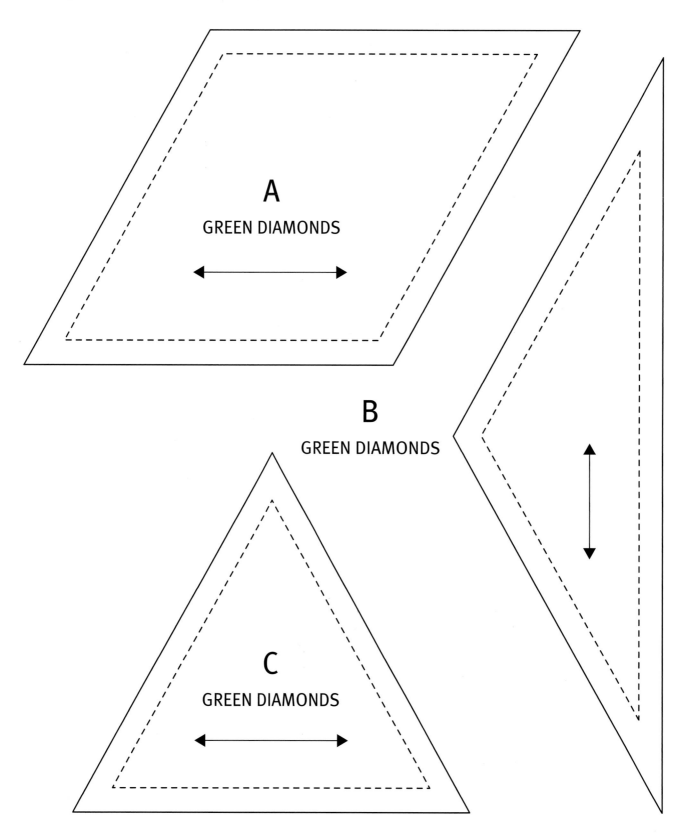

A
GREEN DIAMONDS

B
GREEN DIAMONDS

C
GREEN DIAMONDS

D

GREEN DIAMONDS

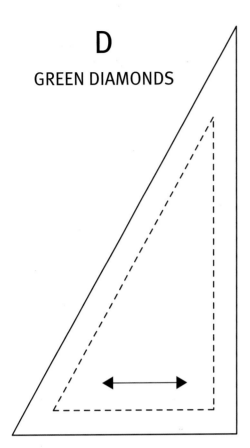

D REVERSE

GREEN DIAMONDS

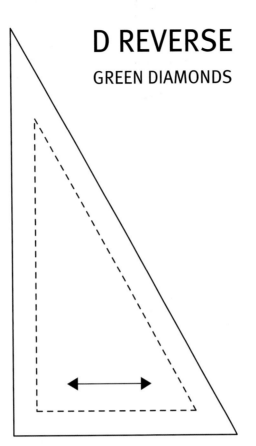

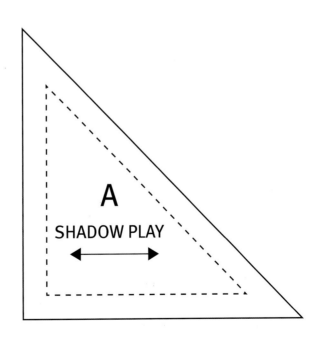

A

SHADOW PLAY

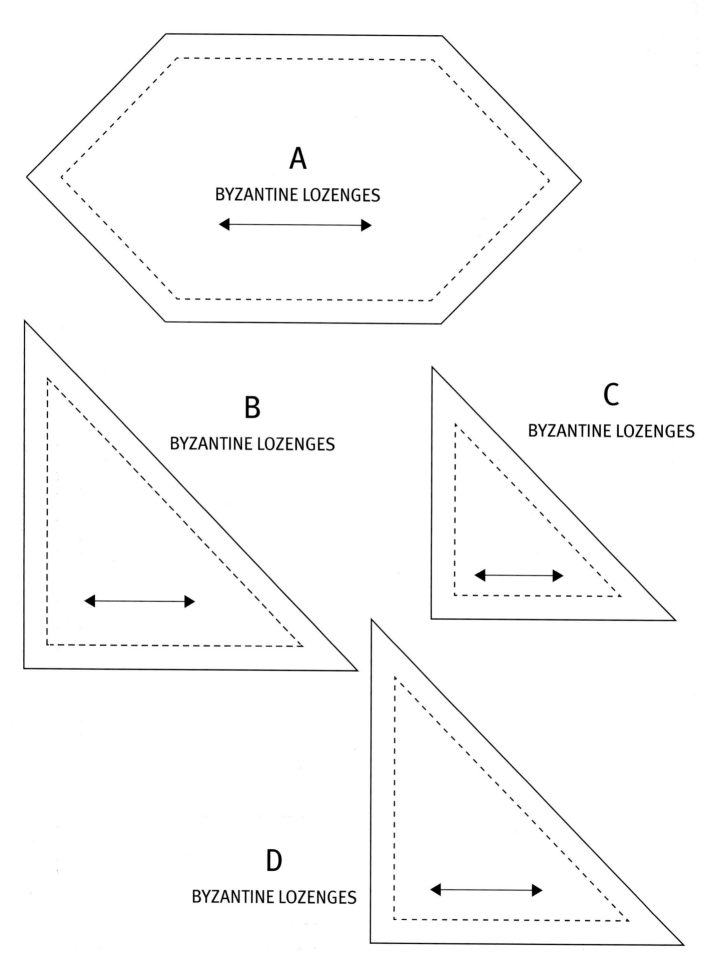

A

BYZANTINE LOZENGES

B

BYZANTINE LOZENGES

C

BYZANTINE LOZENGES

D

BYZANTINE LOZENGES

140

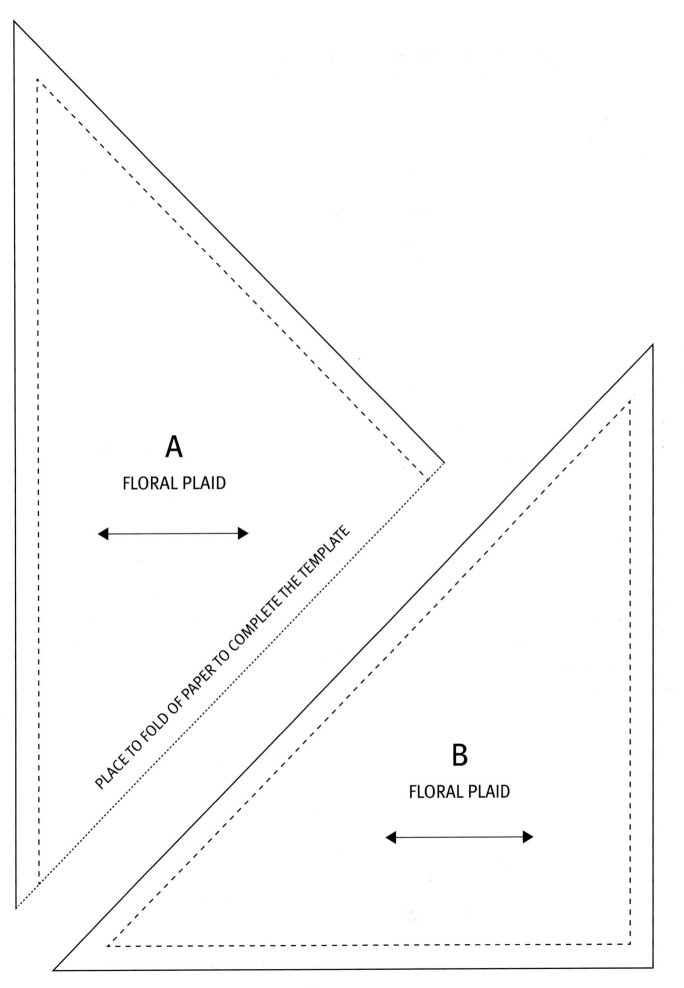

A

FLORAL PLAID

PLACE TO FOLD OF PAPER TO COMPLETE THE TEMPLATE

B

FLORAL PLAID

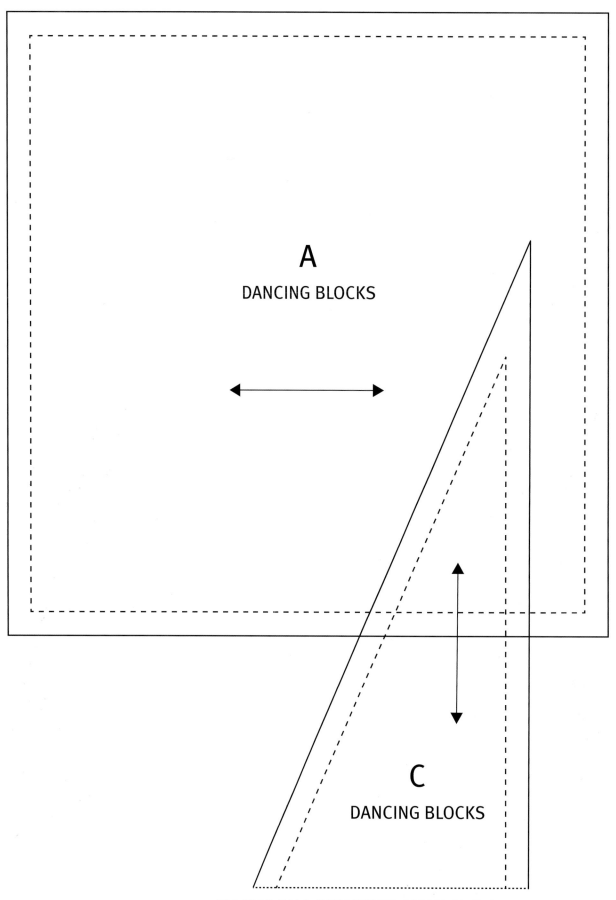

A

DANCING BLOCKS

C

DANCING BLOCKS

PLACE TO FOLD OF PAPER TO COMPLETE THE TEMPLATE

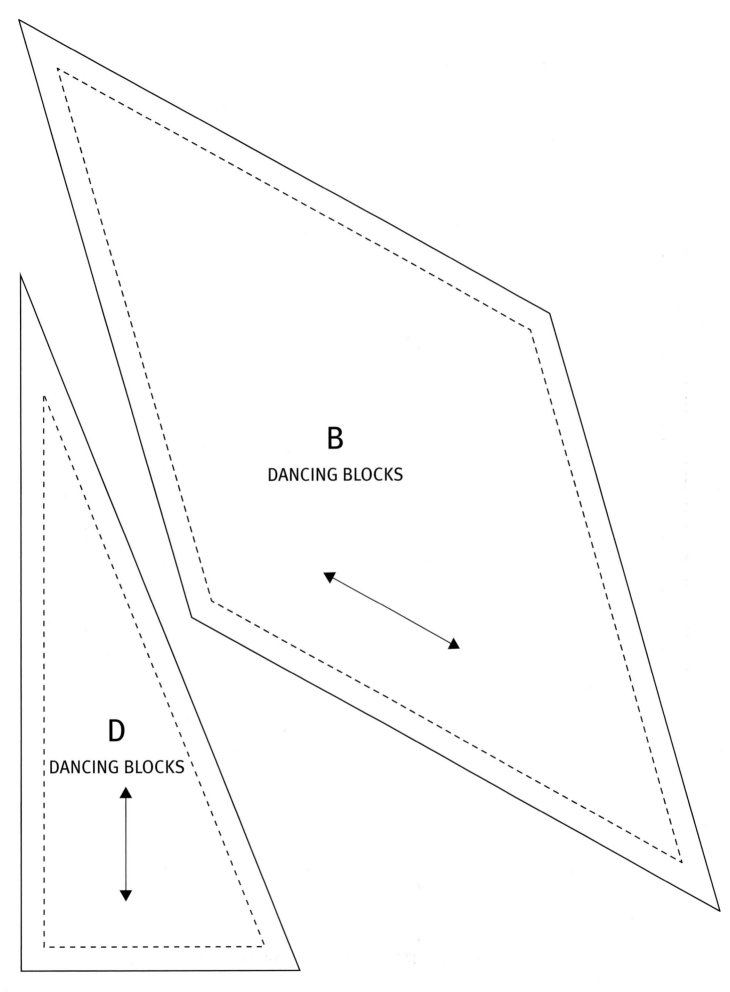

B
DANCING BLOCKS

D
DANCING BLOCKS

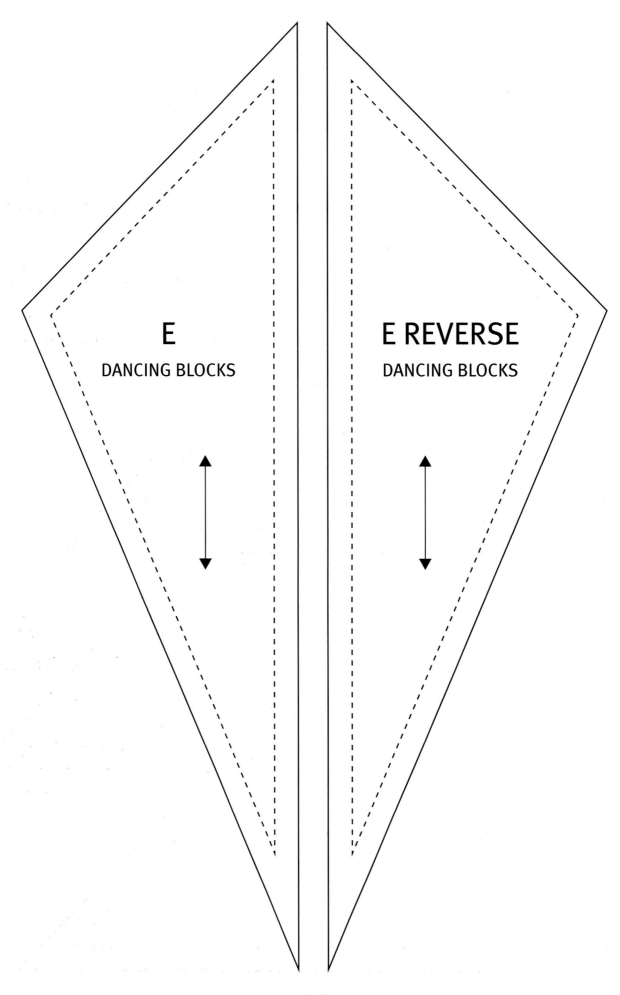

E
DANCING BLOCKS

E REVERSE
DANCING BLOCKS

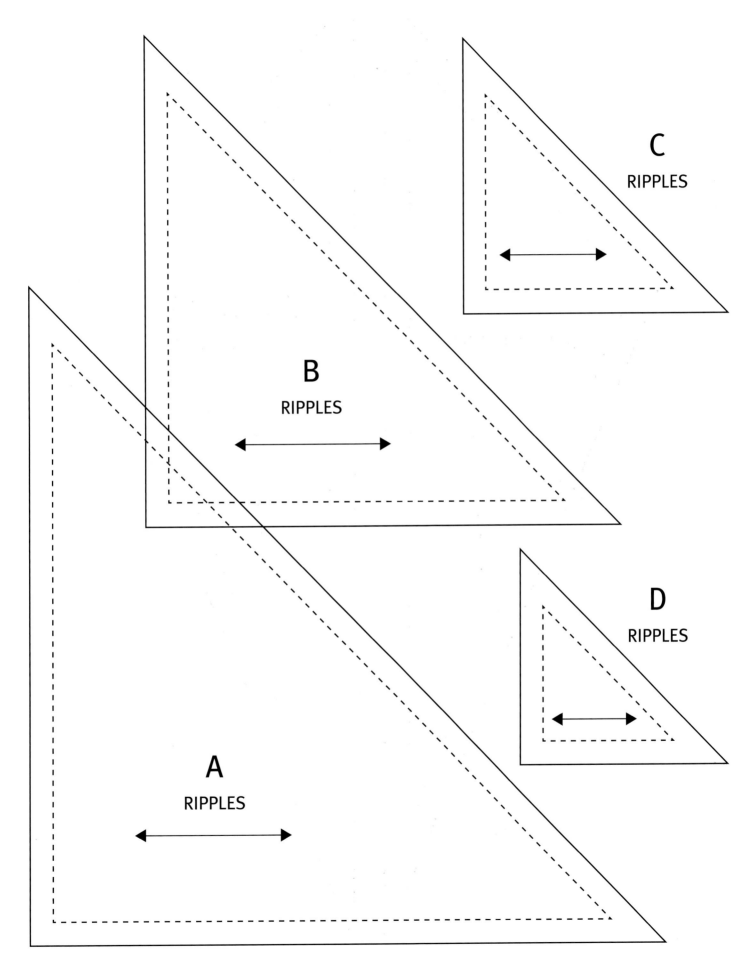

C
RIPPLES

B
RIPPLES

D
RIPPLES

A
RIPPLES

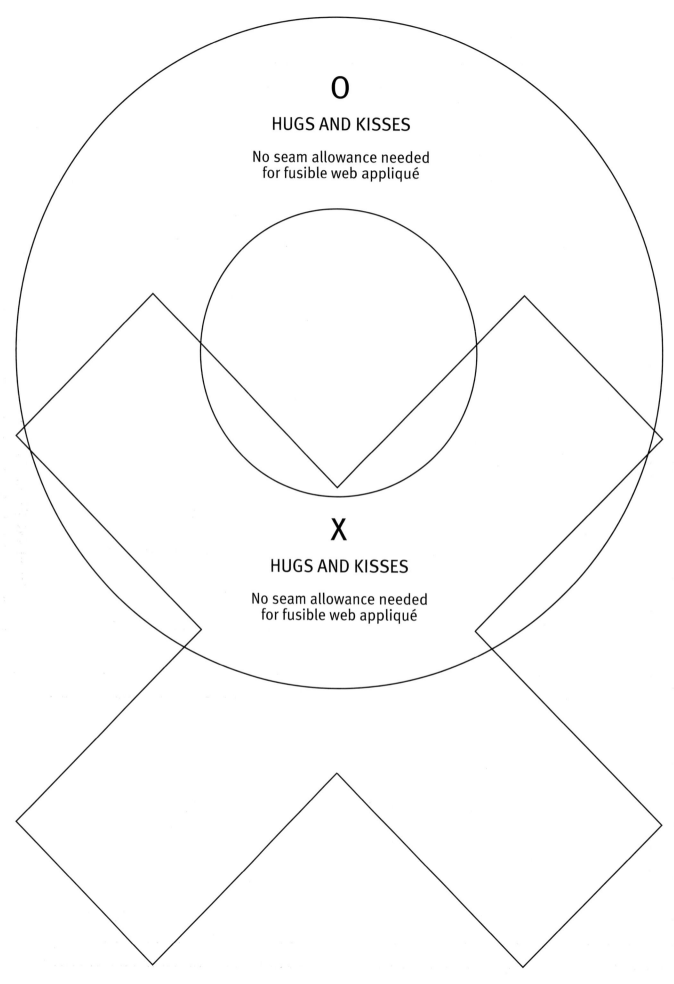

O

HUGS AND KISSES

No seam allowance needed
for fusible web appliqué

X

HUGS AND KISSES

No seam allowance needed
for fusible web appliqué

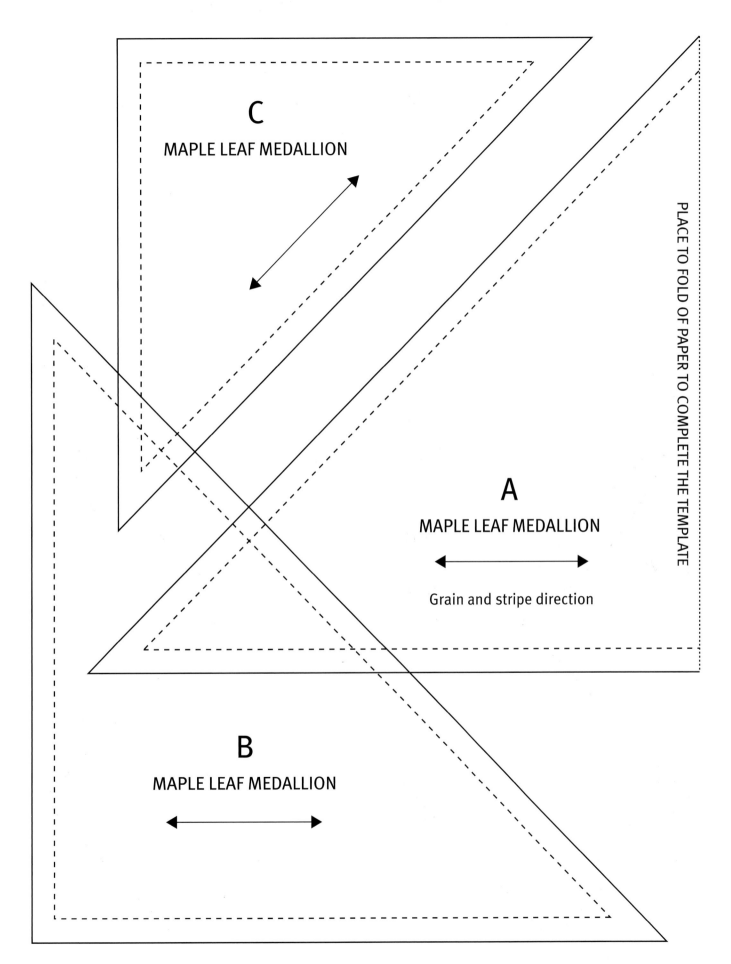

C

MAPLE LEAF MEDALLION

A

MAPLE LEAF MEDALLION

Grain and stripe direction

B

MAPLE LEAF MEDALLION

PLACE TO FOLD OF PAPER TO COMPLETE THE TEMPLATE

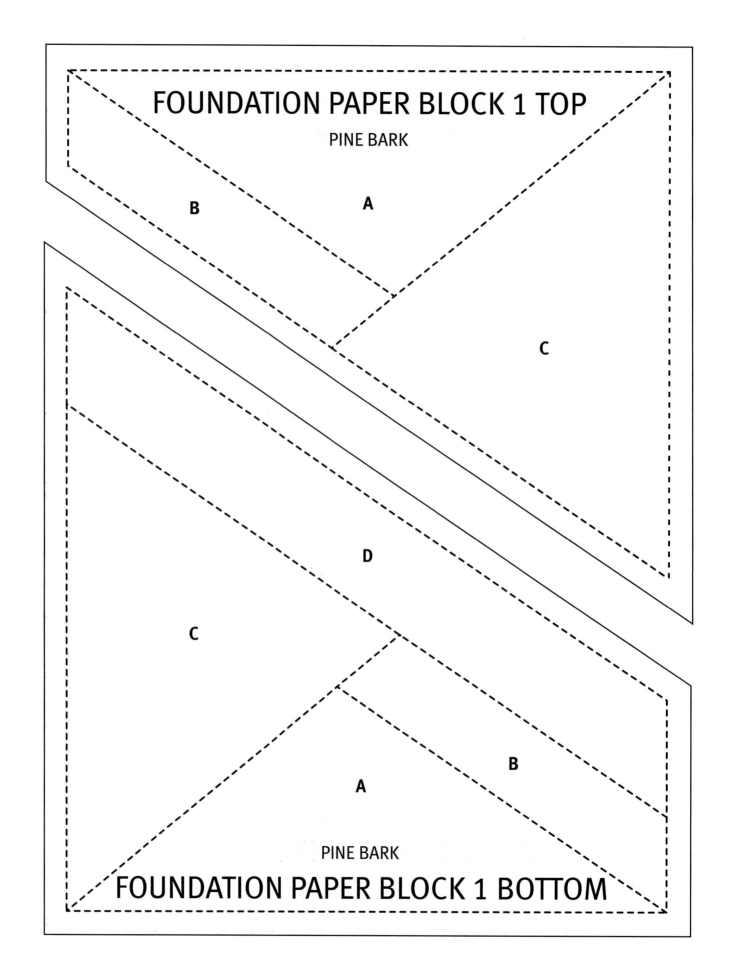

FOUNDATION PAPER BLOCK 1 TOP

PINE BARK

B

A

C

D

C

B

A

PINE BARK

FOUNDATION PAPER BLOCK 1 BOTTOM

Foundation Papers are reversed ready for use

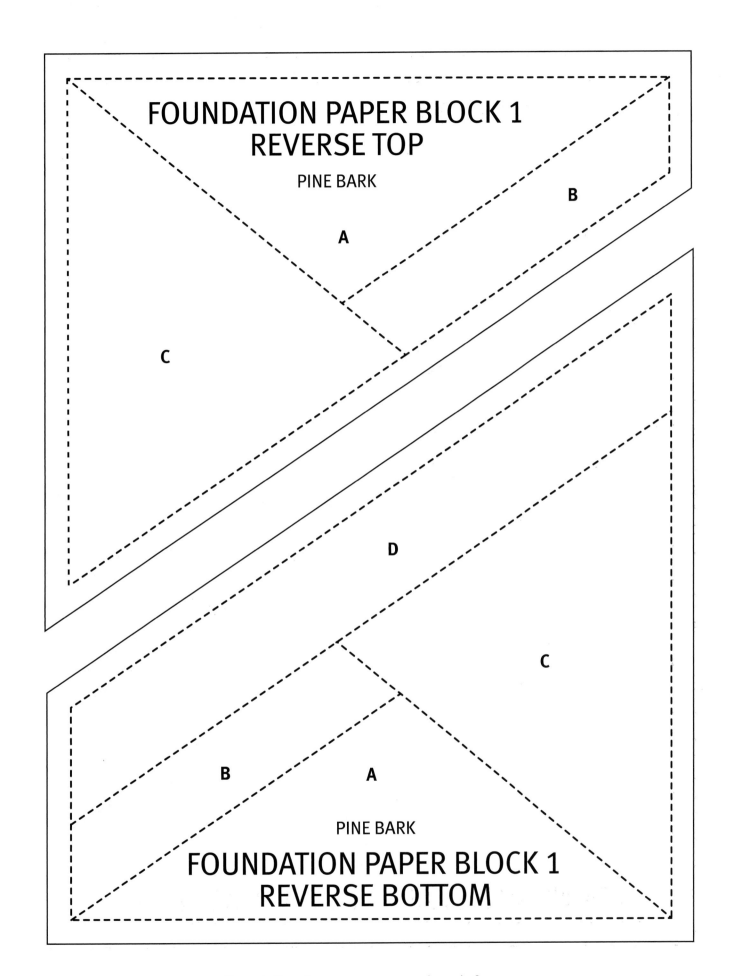

FOUNDATION PAPER BLOCK 1
REVERSE TOP

PINE BARK

A

B

C

D

C

B

A

PINE BARK

FOUNDATION PAPER BLOCK 1
REVERSE BOTTOM

Foundation Papers are reversed ready for use

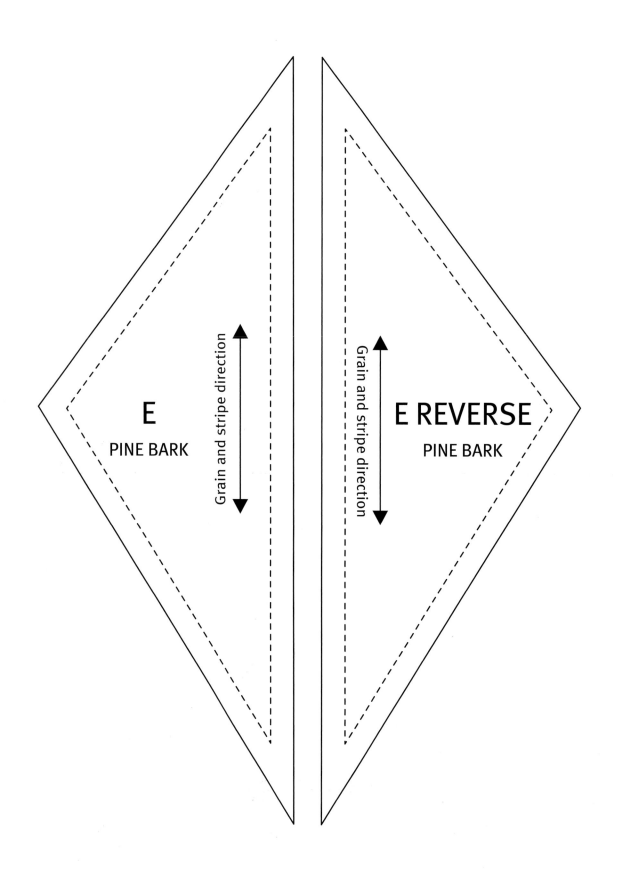

E
PINE BARK

Grain and stripe direction

E REVERSE
PINE BARK

Grain and stripe direction

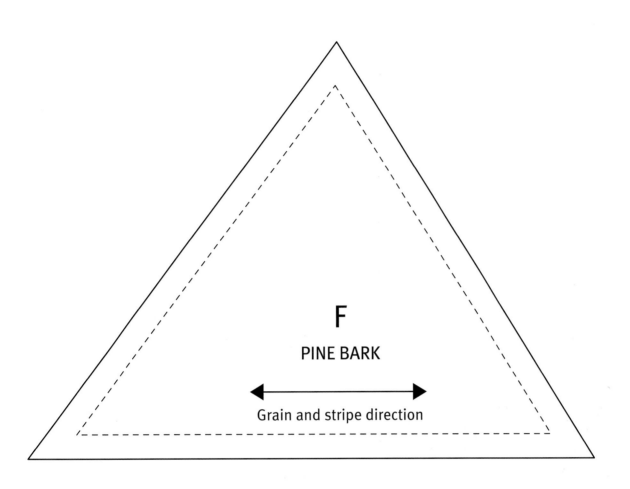

F

PINE BARK

Grain and stripe direction

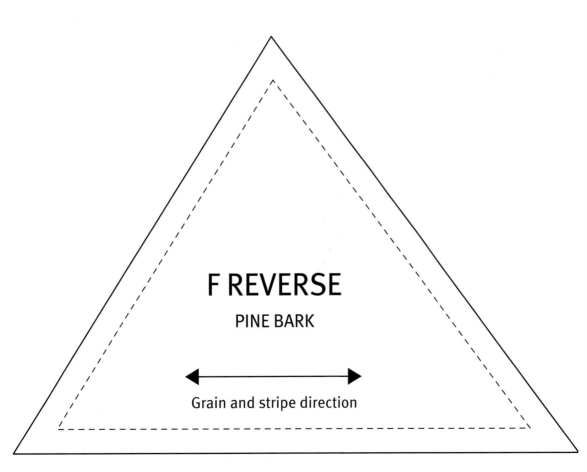

F REVERSE

PINE BARK

Grain and stripe direction

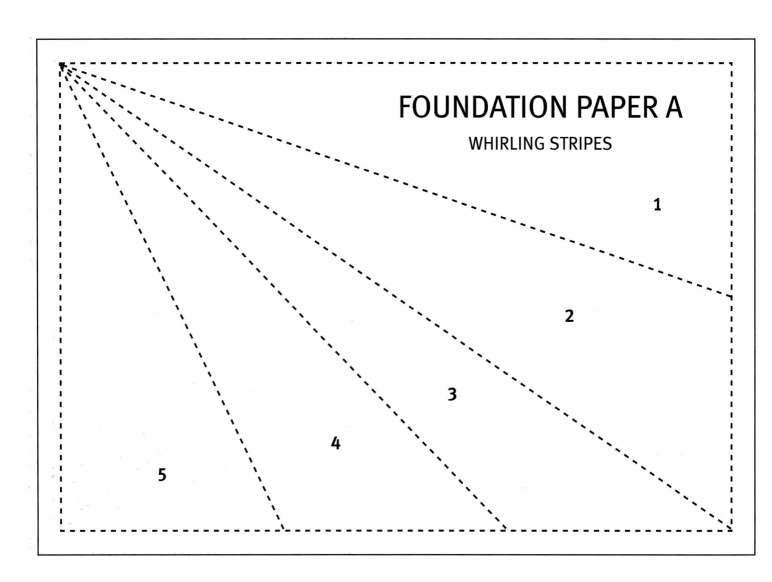

FOUNDATION PAPER A
WHIRLING STRIPES

1

2

3

4

5

Foundation Papers are reversed ready for use

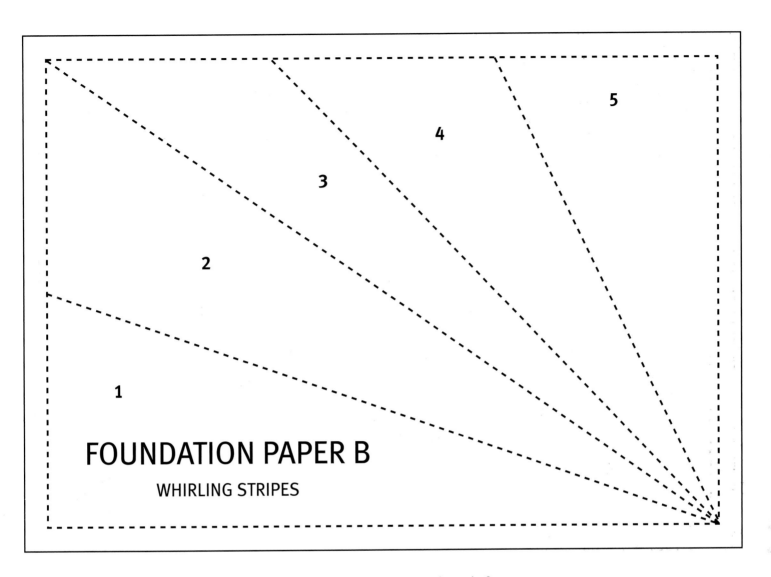

FOUNDATION PAPER B

WHIRLING STRIPES

Foundation Papers are reversed ready for use

patchwork know-how

These instructions are intended for the novice quilt maker, providing the basic information needed to make the projects in this book, along with some useful tips.

EXPERIENCE RATINGS
* Easy, straightforward, suitable for a beginner.
** Suitable for the average patchwork and quilter.
*** For the more experienced patchwork and quilter.

ABOUT THE FABRICS
The fabrics used for the quilts in this book are from Kaffe Fassett Collective. The first two letters of the fabric codes denote the designer:
GP is the code for the Kaffe Fassett collection
PJ is the code for the Philip Jacobs collection
BM is the code for the Brandon Mably collection.

PREPARING THE FABRIC
Prewash all new fabrics before you begin, to ensure that there will be no uneven shrinkage and no bleeding of colours when the finished quilt is laundered. Press the fabric whilst it is still damp to return crispness to it. All fabric requirements in this book are calculated on a 40in (101.5cm) usable fabric width, to allow for shrinkage and selvedge removal.

MAKING TEMPLATES
Transparent template plastic is the best material to use: it is durable and allows you to see the fabric and select certain motifs. You can also use thin stiff cardboard.

Templates for machine piecing
1 Trace off the actual–sized template provided either directly on to template plastic, or tracing paper, and then on to thin cardboard. Use a ruler to help you trace off the straight cutting line, dotted seam line and grain lines.
  Some of the templates in this book were too large to print complete. Transfer the template onto the fold of a large sheet of paper, cut out and open out for the full template.
2 Cut out the traced off template using a craft knife, a ruler and a self–healing cutting mat.
3 Punch holes in the corners of the template, at each point on the seam line, using a hole punch.

Templates for hand piecing
• Make a template as for machine piecing, but do not trace off the cutting line. Use the dotted seam line as the outer edge of the template.

• This template allows you to draw the seam lines directly on to the fabric. The seam allowances can then be cut by eye around the patch.

CUTTING THE FABRIC
On the individual instructions for each project, you will find a summary of all the patch shapes used.
  Always mark and cut out any border and binding strips first, followed by the largest patch shapes and finally the smallest ones, to make the most efficient use of your fabric. The border and binding strips are best cut using a rotary cutter.

Rotary cutting
Rotary cut strips are usually cut across the fabric from selvedge to selvedge, but some projects may vary, so please read through all the instructions before you start cutting the fabrics.

1 Before beginning to cut, press out any folds or creases in the fabric. If you are cutting a large piece of fabric, you will need to fold it several times to fit the cutting mat. When there is only a single fold, place the fold facing you. If the fabric is too wide to be folded only once, fold it concertina-style until it fits your mat. A small rotary cutter with a sharp blade will cut up to six layers of fabric; a large cutter up to eight layers.

2 To ensure that your cut strips are straight and even, the folds must be placed exactly parallel to the straight edges of the fabric and along a line on the cutting mat.

3 Place a plastic ruler over the raw edge of the fabric, overlapping it about ½in (1.25cm). Make sure that the ruler is at right angles to both the straight edges and the fold to ensure that you cut along the straight grain. Press down on the ruler and wheel the cutter away from you along the edge of the ruler.

4 Open out the fabric to check the edge. Don't worry if it's not perfectly straight – a little wiggle will not show when the quilt is stitched together. Re-fold fabric, then place the ruler over the trimmed edge, aligning the edge with the markings on the ruler that match the correct strip width. Cut strip along the edge of the ruler.

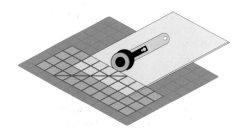

USING TEMPLATES
The most efficient way to cut out templates is by first rotary cutting a strip of fabric to the width stated for your template, and then marking off your templates along the strip, edge to edge at the required angle. This method leaves hardly any waste and gives a random effect to your patches.
  A less efficient method is to 'fussy cut' them, where the templates are cut individually by placing them on particular motifs or stripes, to create special effects. Although this method is more wasteful, it yields very interesting results.

1 Place the template face down, on the wrong side of the fabric, with the grain-line arrow following the straight grain of the fabric, if indicated. Be careful though – check with your individual instructions, as some instructions may ask you to cut patches on varying grains.

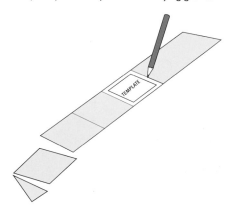

2 Hold the template firmly in place and draw around it with a sharp pencil or crayon, marking in the corner dots or seam lines. To save fabric, position patches close together or even touching. Don't worry if outlines positioned on the straight grain when drawn on striped fabrics do not always match the stripes when cut – this will add a degree of visual excitement to the patchwork!

3 Once you've drawn all the pieces needed, you are ready to cut the fabric, with either a rotary cutter and ruler or a pair of sharp sewing scissors.

BASIC HAND AND MACHINE PIECING
Patches can be stitched together by hand or machine. Machine stitching is quicker, but hand assembly allows you to carry your patches around with you and work on them in every spare moment. The choice is yours. For techniques that are new to you, practise on scrap pieces of fabric until you feel confident.

Machine piecing

Follow the quilt instructions for the order in which to piece the individual patchwork blocks and then assemble the blocks together in rows.

1 Seam lines are not marked on the fabric for simple shapes, so stitch ¼in (6mm) seams using the machine needle plate, a ¼in (6mm) wide machine foot, or tape stuck to the machine as a guide. Pin two patches with right sides together, matching edges.

For some shapes, particularly diamonds, you need to match the sewing lines, not the fabric edges. Place 2 diamonds right sides together but offset so that the sewing lines intersect at the correct position. Use pins to secure for sewing.

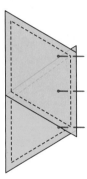

Set your machine at 10–12 stitches per inch (2.5cm) and stitch seams from edge to edge, removing pins as you feed the fabric through the machine.

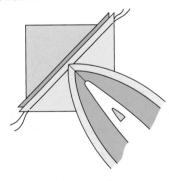

2 Press the seams of each patchwork block to one side before attempting to join it to another block. When joining diamond shaped blocks you will need to offset the blocks in the same way as diamond shaped patches, matching the sewing lines, not the fabric edges.

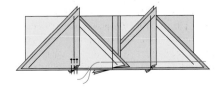

3 When joining rows of blocks, make sure that adjacent seam allowances are pressed in opposite directions to reduce bulk and make matching easier. Pin pieces together directly through the stitch line and to the right and left of the seam. Remove pins as you sew. Continue pressing seams to one side as you work.

Hand piecing

1 Pin two patches with right sides together, so that the marked seam lines are facing outwards.

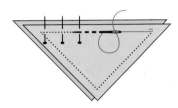

2 Using a single strand of strong thread, secure the corner of a seam line with a couple of back stitches.

3 Sew running stitches along the marked line, working 8–10 stitches per inch (2.5cm) and ending at the opposite seam line corner with a few back stitches. When hand piecing never stitch over the seam allowances.

4 Press the seams to one side, as shown in machine piecing (Step 2).

MACHINE APPLIQUÉ WITH ADHESIVE WEB

To make appliqué very easy you can use adhesive web (which comes attached to a paper backing sheet) to bond the motifs to the background fabric. There are two types of web available: the first keeps the pieces in place while they are stitched, the second permanently attaches the pieces so that no sewing is required. Follow steps 1 and 2 for the non-sew type and steps 1–3 for the type that requires sewing.

1 Trace the reversed appliqué design onto the paper side of the adhesive web leaving a ¼in (6mm) gap between all the shapes. Roughly cut out the motifs ⅛in (3mm) outside your drawn line.

2 Bond the motifs to the reverse of your chosen fabrics. Cut out on the drawn line with very sharp scissors. Remove the backing paper by scoring the centre of the motif carefully with a scissor point and peeling the paper away from the centre out (to prevent damage to the edges). Place the motifs onto the background, noting any which may be layered. Cover with a clean cloth and bond with a hot iron (check instructions for temperature setting as adhesive web can vary depending on the manufacturer).

3 Using a contrasting or toning coloured thread in your machine, work small close zigzag stitches (or a blanket stitch if your machine has one) around the edge of the motifs; the majority of the stitching should sit on the appliqué shape. When stitching up to points stop with the machine needle in the down position, lift the foot of your machine, pivot the work, lower the foot and continue to stitch. Make sure all the raw edges are stitched.

HAND APPLIQUÉ

Good preparation is essential for speedy and accurate hand appliqué. The finger-pressing method is suitable for needle-turning application, used for simple shapes like leaves and flowers. Using a card template is the best method for bold simple motifs such as circles.

Finger–pressing method

1 To make your template, transfer the appliqué design using carbon paper on to stiff card, and cut out the template. Trace around the outline of your appliquéd shape on to the right side of your fabric using a well sharpened pencil. Cut out shapes, adding by eye a ¼in (6mm) seam allowance all around.

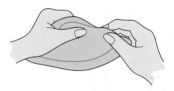

2 Hold shape right side up and fold under the seam, turning along your drawn line, pinch to form a crease. Dampening the fabric makes this very easy. When using shapes with 'points' such as leaves, turn in the seam allowance at the 'point' first, as shown in the diagram. Then continue all round the shape. If your shapes have sharp curves, you can snip the seam allowance to ease the curve. Take care not to stretch the appliqué shapes as you work.

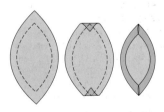

Straight stems

Place fabric face down and simply press over the ¼in (6mm) seam allowance along each edge. You don't need to finish the ends of stems that are layered under other appliqué shapes. Where the end of the stem is visible, simply tuck under the end and finish neatly.

Needle-turning application

Take the appliqué shape and pin in position. Stroke the seam allowance under with the tip of the needle as far as the creased pencil line, and hold securely in place with your thumb. Using a matching thread, bring the needle up from the back of the block into the edge of the shape and proceed to blind-hem in place. (This stitch allows the motifs to appear to be held on invisibly.) To do this, bring the thread out from below through the folded edge of the motif, never on the top. The stitches must be small, even and close together to prevent the seam allowance from unfolding and from frayed edges appearing. Try to avoid pulling the stitches too tight, as this will cause the motifs to pucker up. Work around the whole shape, stroking under each small section before sewing.

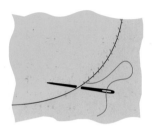

QUILTING
When you have finished piecing your patchwork and added any borders, press it carefully. It is now ready for quilting.

Marking quilting designs and motifs
Many tools are available for marking quilting patterns, check the manufacturer's instructions for use and test on scraps of fabric from your project. Use an acrylic ruler for marking straight lines.

Stencils
Some designs require stencils, these can be made at home, by transferring the designs on to template plastic, or stiff cardboard. The design is then cut away in the form of long dashes, to act as guides for both internal and external lines. These stencils are a quick method for producing an identical set of repeated designs.

BACKING FABRIC
The quilts in this book use two different widths of backing fabric – the standard width of 44in (112cm) and a wider one of 108in (274cm). If you can't find (or don't want to use) the wider fabric then select a standard-width fabric instead and adjust the amount accordingly. For most of the quilts in the book, using a standard-width fabric will probably mean joins in the fabric. The material list for each quilt assumes that an extra 4in of backing fabric is needed all round (8in in total) when making up the quilt sandwich, to allow for long-arm quilting if needed. We have assumed a usable width of 40in (102cm), to allow for selvedge removal and possible shrinkage after washing.

Preparing the backing and batting
• Remove the selvedges and piece together the backing fabric to form a backing at least 4in (10cm) larger all round than the patchwork top.

• Choose a fairly thin batting, preferably pure cotton, to give your quilt a flat appearance. If your batting has been rolled up, unroll it and let it rest before cutting it to the same size as the backing.

• For a large quilt it may be necessary to join two pieces of batting to fit. Lay the pieces of batting on a flat surface so that they overlap by around 8in (20cm). Cut a curved line through both layers.

overlap wadding

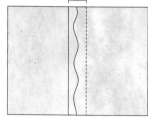

• Carefully peel away the two narrow pieces and discard. Butt the curved cut edges back together. Stitch the two pieces together using a large herringbone stitch.

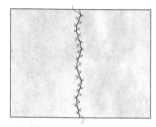

BASTING THE LAYERS TOGETHER
1 On the floor or on a large work surface, lay out the backing with wrong side uppermost. Use weights along the edges to keep it taut.

2 Lay the batting on the backing and smooth it out gently. Next lay the patchwork top, right side up, on top of the batting and smooth gently until there are no wrinkles. Pin at the corners and at the midpoints of each side, close to the edges.

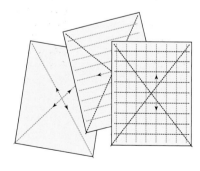

3 Beginning at the centre, baste diagonal lines outwards to the corners, making your stitches about 3in (7.5cm) long. Then, again starting at the centre, baste horizontal and vertical lines out to the edges. Continue basting until you have basted a grid of lines about 4in (10cm) apart over the entire quilt.

4 For speed, when machine quilting, some quilters prefer to baste their quilt sandwich layers together using rust-proof safety pins, spaced at 4in (10cm) intervals over the entire quilt.

HAND QUILTING
This is best done with the quilt mounted on a quilting frame or hoop, but as long as you have basted the quilt well, a frame is not essential. With the quilt top facing upwards, begin at the centre of the quilt and make even running stitches following the design. It is more important to make even stitches on both sides of the quilt than to make small ones. Start and finish your stitching with back stitches and bury the ends of your threads in the batting.

TIED QUILTING
The Pine Bark quilt uses hand quilting and tied quilting, rather than machine quilting. For tied quilting, use a strong thread that will withstand being pulled through the quilt layers and tied in a knot. You can tie with the knot on the front of the quilt or the back, as preferred. Leaving tufts of thread gives an attractive, rustic look.

Thread a needle with a suitable thread, using the number of strands noted in the project. Put the needle and thread through from the front of the work, leaving a long tail. Go through to the back of the quilt, make a small stitch and then come back through to the front. Tie the threads together using a reef knot and trim the thread ends to the desired length. For extra security, you could tie a double knot or add a spot of fabric glue on the knot.

MACHINE QUILTING

• For a flat looking quilt, always use a walking foot on your machine for stitching straight lines, and a darning foot for free–motion quilting.

• It is best to start your quilting at the centre of the quilt and work out towards the borders, doing the straight quilting lines first (stitch-in-the-ditch) followed by the free-motion quilting.

• When free motion-quilting stitch in a loose meandering style as shown in the diagrams. Do not stitch too closely as this will make the quilt feel stiff when finished. If you wish you can include floral themes or follow shapes on the printed fabrics for added interest.

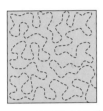

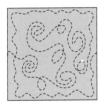

• Make it easier for yourself by handling the quilt properly. Roll up the excess quilt neatly to fit under your sewing machine arm, and use a table or chair to help support the weight of the quilt that hangs down the other side.

FINISHING

Preparing to bind the edges

Once you have quilted or tied your quilt sandwich together, remove all the basting stitches. Then, baste around the outer edge of the quilt ¼in (6mm) from the edge of the top patchwork layer. Trim the back and batting to the edge of the patchwork and straighten the edge of the patchwork if necessary.

Making the binding

1 Cut bias or straight grain strips the width required for your binding, making sure the grain-line is running the correct way on your straight grain strips. Cut enough strips until you have the required length to go around the edge of your quilt.

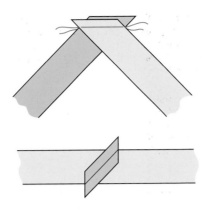

2 To join strips together, the two ends that are to be joined must be cut at a 45 degree angle, as above. Stitch right sides together, trim turnings and press seam open.

Binding the edges

1 Cut the starting end of binding strip at a 45 degree angle, fold a ¼in (6mm) turning to wrong side along cut edge and press in place. With wrong sides together, fold strip in half lengthways, keeping raw edges level, and press.

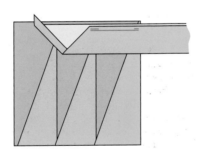

2 Starting at the centre of one of the long edges, place the doubled binding on to the right side of the quilt keeping raw edges level. Stitch the binding in place starting ¼in (6mm) in from the diagonal folded edge. Reverse stitch to secure, and work ¼in (6mm) in from edge of the quilt towards first corner of quilt. Stop ¼in (6mm) in from corner and work a few reverse stitches.

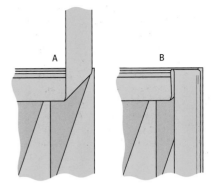

3 Fold the loose end of the binding up, making a 45 degree angle (see A). Keeping the diagonal fold in place, fold the binding back down, aligning the raw edges with the next side of the quilt. Starting at the point where the last stitch ended, stitch down the next side (see B).

4 Continue to stitch the binding in place around all the quilt edges in this way, tucking the finishing end of the binding inside the diagonal starting section.

5 Turn the folded edge of the binding on to the back of the quilt. Hand stitch the folded edge in place just covering binding machine stitches, and folding a mitre at each corner

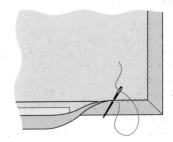

glossary of terms

Adhesive or fusible web This comes attached to a paper backing sheet and is used to bond appliqué motifs to a background fabric. There are 2 types of web available, the first keeps the pieces in place whilst they are stitched, the second permanently attaches the pieces so that no sewing is required.

Appliqué The technique of stitching fabric shapes on to a background to create a design. It can be applied either by hand or machine with a decorative embroidery stitch, such as buttonhole, or satin stitch.

Backing The bottom layer of a quilt sandwich. It is made of fabric pieced to the size of the quilt top with the addition of about 4in (10.25cm) all around to allow for quilting take-up.

Basting or tacking This is a means of holding two fabric layers or the layers of a quilt sandwich together temporarily with large hand stitches, or pins.

Batting or wadding This is the middle layer, or padding in a quilt. It can be made of cotton, wool, silk or synthetic fibres.

Bias The diagonal grain of a fabric. This is the direction which has the most give or stretch, making it ideal for bindings, especially on curved edges.

Binding A narrow strip of fabric used to finish off the edges of quilts or projects; it can be cut on the straight grain of a fabric or on the bias.

Block A single design unit that when stitched together with other blocks create the quilt top. It is most often a square, hexagon, or rectangle, but it can be any shape. It can be pieced or plain.

Border A frame of fabric stitched to the outer edges of the quilt top. Borders can be narrow or wide, pieced or plain. As well as making the quilt larger, they unify the overall design and draw attention to the central area.

Chalk pencils Available in various colours, they are used for marking lines, or spots on fabric.

Cutting mat Designed for use with a rotary cutter, it is made from a special 'self–healing' material that keeps your cutting blade sharp. Cutting mats come in various sizes and are usually marked with a grid to help you line up the edges of fabric and cut out larger pieces.

Design wall Used for laying out fabric patches before sewing. A large wall or folding board covered with flannel fabric or cotton batting in a neutral shade (dull beige or grey work well) will hold fabric in place so that an overall view can be taken of the placement.

Free-motion quilting Curved wavy quilting lines stitched in a random manner. Stitching diagrams are often given for you to follow as a loose guide.

Fussy cutting This is when a template is placed on a particular motif, or stripe, to obtain interesting effects. This method is not as efficient as strip cutting, but yields very interesting results.

Grain The direction in which the threads run in a woven fabric. In a vertical direction it is called the lengthwise grain, which has very little stretch. The horizontal direction, or crosswise grain is slightly stretchy, but diagonally the fabric has a lot of stretch. This grain is called the bias. Wherever possible the grain of a fabric should run in the same direction on a quilt block and borders.

Grain lines These are arrows printed on templates which should be aligned with the fabric grain.

Inset seams or setting-in A patchwork technique whereby one patch (or block) is stitched into a 'V' shape formed by the joining of two other patches (or blocks).

Patch A small shaped piece of fabric used in the making of a patchwork pattern.

Patchwork The technique of stitching small pieces of fabric (patches) together to create a larger piece of fabric, usually forming a design.

Pieced quilt A quilt composed of patches.

Quilting Traditionally done by hand with running stitches, but for speed modern quilts are often stitched by machine. The stitches are sewn through the top, wadding and backing to hold the three layers together. Quilting stitches are usually worked in some form of design, but they can be random.

Quilting hoop Consists of two wooden circular or oval rings with a screw adjuster on the outer ring. It stabilises the quilt layers, helping to create an even tension.

Reducing Glass Used for viewing the complete composition of a quilt at a glance. It works like a magnifier in reverse. A useful tool for checking fabric placement before piecing a quilt.

Rotary cutter A sharp circular blade attached to a handle for quick, accurate cutting. It is a device that can be used to cut several layers of fabric at one time. It must be used in conjunction with a 'self–healing' cutting mat and a thick plastic ruler.

Rotary ruler A thick, clear plastic ruler marked with lines in imperial or metric measurements. Sometimes they also have diagonal lines indicating 45 and 60 degree angles. A rotary ruler is used as a guide when cutting out fabric pieces using a rotary cutter.

Sashing A piece or pieced sections of fabric interspaced between blocks.

Sashing posts When blocks have sashing between them the corner squares are known as sashing posts.

Selvedges Also known as selvages, these are the firmly woven edges down each side of a fabric length. Selvedges should be trimmed off before cutting out your fabric, as they are more liable to shrink when the fabric is washed.

Stitch-in-the-ditch or Ditch quilting Also known as quilting-in-the-ditch. The quilting stitches are worked along the actual seam lines, to give a pieced quilt texture.

Template A pattern piece used as a guide for marking and cutting out fabric patches, or marking a quilting, or appliqué design. Usually made from plastic or strong card that can be reused many times. Templates for cutting fabric usually have marked grain lines which should be aligned with the fabric grain.

Threads One hundred percent cotton or cotton–covered polyester is best for hand and machine piecing. Choose a colour that matches your fabric. When sewing different colours and patterns together, choose a medium to light neutral colour, such as grey or ecru. Specialist quilting threads are available for hand and machine quilting.

Walking foot or Quilting foot This is a sewing machine foot with dual feed control. It is very helpful when quilting, as the fabric layers are fed evenly from the top and below, reducing the risk of slippage and puckering.

Yo-Yos A circle of fabric double the size of the finished puff is gathered up into a rosette shape.

ACKNOWLEDGMENTS

These books are always the product of a lot of co-operation so I'm happy to have the chance to thank Judy Brittain for guiding us round her wonderful part of Ireland and for hosting us so graciously.

Thanks so much to all those generous people who allowed us to use their establishments to show off our quilts, in particular to Thomas Lawlee, the owner of Fresh Start greengrocers, and Barron's Bakery, and to the owners of Glenville Park.

My gratitude goes out to Heart Space Studios for coordinating the making of my own quilts (by Ilaria Padovani and Julie Harvey) and to Liza Lucy for co-ordinating the American quiltmaking. Last but not least to Debbie Patterson, our ever faithful photographer for her patience, good nature and sharp eye, and to Brandon Mably for overseeing the location photography project. And, as ever, to all the other members of the team.

OTHER TAUNTON TITLES AVAILABLE

Kaffe Fassett's Quilt Romance
Kaffe Fassett's Quilts en Provence
Kaffe Fassett's Quilts in Sweden
Kaffe Quilts Again
Kaffe Fassett's Quilt Grandeur
Kaffe Fassett's Quilts in Morocco
Kaffe Fassett's Heritage Quilts
Kaffe Fassett's Quilts in Italy

The fabric collection can be viewed online at
www.freespiritfabrics.com

The Taunton Press
Inspiration for hands-on living®

The Taunton Press, Inc., 63 South Main Street,
P.O. Box 5506, Newtown, CT 06470-5506
Tel: 800-888-8286 • Email: tp@taunton.com
www.tauntonstore.com

KAFFE FASSETT

——————— for ———————

Free Spirit

Westminster Fibers, Inc., 3430 Toringdon Way, Suite 301,
Charlotte, NC 28277, U.S.A.
(866) 907-3305 (US & Canada only)
Email: kimberly.porter@westminsterfibers.com
www.freespiritfabrics.com

distributors and stockists

To find a retailer in the USA and
Canada, please go to
www.freespiritfabrics.com

For the following countries, see
contact information below:

AUSTRALIA
XLN Fabrics
2/21 Binney Rd
Kings Park
NSW 2148
www.xln.com.au
email: allanmurphy@xln.com.au

**CHINA (inc HONG KONG/MACAO/
TAIWAN)**
Wan Mei Di China
502 CaoXi Rd (N)
Xuhui District
Shanghai
China
email: 12178550@qq.com

EUROPE (SEE UK/EUROPE)

HONG KONG
Wan Mei Di China
502 CaoXi Rd (N)
Xuhui District
Shanghai
China
email: 12178550@qq.com

JAPAN
Kiyohara & Co Ltd
4-5-2 Minamikyuhoji-machi Chuo-ku
Osaka 541-8506
www. kiyohara.co.jp
aemail: Kazuo.fujii@kiyohara.co.jp

KOREA
Young Do Trimart Co Ltd
6th floor Dongwon Building
458 Cheonggyecheon-ro
Seongdong-gu
Seoul
www.youndoco.tradekorea.com
email: Trade1@youngdo.co.kr

MACAO
Wan Mei Di China
502 CaoXi Rd (N)
Xuhui District
Shanghai
China
email: 12178550@qq.com

NEW ZEALAND
Fabco Ltd
280 School Road
Muriwai Valley 0881
www.fabco.co.nz
melanie@fabco.co.nz

SOUTH AFRICA
Arthur Bales Pty Ltd
62 4th Avenue
Johannesburg 2104
www.arthurbales.co.za
email: nicci@arthurbales.co.za

TAIWAN
Long Teh Trading Co Ltd
71 Hebei W. St
Tai Chung 40669
email: Longteh.quilt@gmail.com

Wan Mei Diy China
502 CaoXi Rd (N)
Xuhui District
Shanghai
China
email: 12178550@qq.com

UK/EUROPE
Rhinetex
Geurdeland 7
6673 DR Andelst
Netherlands
www.rhinetex.com
email: info@rhinetex.com

MEZ Gmbh
Kaiserstrasse 1
79341 Kenzingen
Germany
www.mezcrafts.de
email: kenzingen.vertrieb@
mezcrafts.com